Legends *of* Animation

Matt
Groening

Legends of Animation

Tex Avery:
Hollywood's Master of Screwball Cartoons

Walt Disney:
The Mouse that Roared

Matt Groening:
From Spitballs to Springfield

William Hanna and Joseph Barbera:
The Sultans of Saturday Morning

Legends *of* Animation

Matt
Groening

From Spitballs to Springfield

Jeff Lenburg

CHELSEA HOUSE
An Infobase Learning Company

Matt Groening: From Spitballs to Springfield

Chelsea House
An Infobase Learning Company
132 West 31st Street
New York NY 10001

Library of Congress Cataloging-in-Publication Data
Lenburg, Jeff.
  Matt Groening : From Spitballs to Springfield / Jeff Lenburg. — First Edition.
      pages cm. — (Legends of Animation)
  Includes bibliographical references and index.
  ISBN-13: 978-1-60413-838-2 (hardcover : alk. paper)
  ISBN-10: 1-60413-838-6 (hardcover : alk. paper) 1. Groening, Matt (Matthew Abram), 1954—Juvenile literature. 2. Animators—United States—Biography—Juvenile literature. I. Title. II. Series.
  NC1766.U52 G735
  741.5'973—dc22
  [B]   2010051746

Chelsea House books are available at special discounts when purchased in bulk quantities for businesses, associations, institutions, or sales promotions. Please call our Special Sales Department in New York at (212) 967-8800 or (800) 322-8755.

You can find Chelsea House on the World Wide Web at
http://www.infobaselearning.com

Text design by Kerry Casey
Cover design by Takeshi Takahashi
Composition by EJB Publishing Services
Cover printed by Yurchak Printing, Landisville, Pa.
Book printed and bound by Yurchak Printing, Landisville, Pa.
Date printed: April 2011   3188

Printed in the United States of America

10 9 8 7 6 5 4 3 2 1

This book is printed on acid-free paper.

To my friend and original "Gangster of Love," Allen "KTRZ" Tarzwell,
for all the laughter, music, fellowship, and roads traveled,
this one is especially for you.

CONTENTS

ACKNOWLEDGMENTS

I would like to personally thank many individuals and organizations for their kindness and generosity in providing many specific insights, details, and information helpful to the biographer in writing this illuminating volume on one of the great artistic and cultural figures of our times.

My sincere thanks to the staffs of the Margaret Herrick Library of the Academy of Motion Picture Arts and Sciences; the Archives of Performing Arts and the Regional History Collections at the University of Southern California; Arizona State University Fletcher Library; the Los Angeles Times Photographic Archive of the University of California, Los Angeles Library; Associated Press; United Press International; Wire Image; the Oregon Historical Society; and many others for the use of books, articles, research, photographs, and other material vital to the success of this project.

My deepest gratitude as well to the following newspapers, the *Los Angeles Daily News*, *Los Angeles Times*, the *New York Times*, the *Oregonian*, the *Olympian*, *Portland Tribune*, *Seattle Post-Intelligencer*, the *Seattle Times*, the *Washington Post*, and the *Wall Street Journal*; popular consumer magazines, *Newsweek*, *People*, and *Time*; and trade publications and journals, *American Film*, *Animation Magazine*, *Emmy*, *Hollywood Reporter*, *Publishers Weekly*, and *Variety* for their extensive coverage of the subject's life and achievements that was of tremendous value.

Finally, to Matt Groening, for your inspiration and positive influence and for showing others seeking their dreams that anything is possible in the face of adversity.

Drawn to Weirdness

O ne day he hoped his fertile imagination and incessant doodling and strong sense of justice and injustice would pay off. Aspiring to become a serious journalist and successful writer, his journey to Hollywood was an inauspicious one. Following a series of disheartening bumps in the roads, cartooning became his claim to fame. Finding Los Angeles a living "hell," he poured his neuroses and pent-up frustrations into creating a comic strip, featuring a "badly" drawn rabbit, that helped pioneer a new wave of alternative comic strips and opened doors for future artists. Then he created a family of lower-middle-class misfits as animated bits for an upstart network's comedy/variety show that led to the high-risk proposition of casting them in television's first prime-time network cartoon series in 30 years.

Now it is nearly impossible to wonder what television would be like today without *The Simpsons*, a subversively humored series that started as its creator's statement on the decline of the American family, or the "real norm" in society, as he called it. Assaulting many time-honored traditions and values as well as cultural absurdities and hypocrisies, he produced the unthinkable: a hit television series. Its staying power stretched far beyond anything he imagined, becoming loved and hated and the target of passionate praise and criticism. From spitballs to Springfield, only one guy could have caused all this commotion and gotten away with it: Matt Groening.

Born on February 15, 1954, and raised in the west hills of Portland, Oregon, Matthew Abram "Matt" Groening (pronounced "gray-ning," or as he once jested, "rhymes with complaining") was the middle child of five children—including brother Mark and sisters Patty, Lisa, and Maggie—raised by his parents, Homer Philip Groening, of German descent, and Norwegian mother Margaret Wiggun, a former schoolteacher. Matt was named in part after his grandfather, Abraham Groening, who was later a professor at Tabor College, a Mennonite Brethren liberal arts college in Hillsboro, Kansas. Of his family lineage, Matt once joked he came from "two of the unfunniest ethnic groups in the history of the world."

The Groenings settled on the Portland area as a suitable place to lay roots. They purchased a five-bedroom, barn-red Cape Cod house on Northwest Evergreen Terrace (where The Simpsons would also live in Matt's fictional cartoon series) to raise their family. Matt's childhood home was a half-mile through densely tree-covered roads from the nearest bus stop and so close to the nearby zoo that he could hear, as he once said, "the lions roaring at night."

Raised in a predominantly Methodist household, Matt grew up conflicted about his faith, an issue that extended into adulthood. When he was 12, during a trip with his Boy Scout troop, he brandished a Gideon Bible from a hotel and, in his words, "marked up all of the dirty bits." His scoutmaster became so outraged that he ejected him from the troop. Matt prayed to God about the incident this way: "I know you'll forgive me for not believing in you."

Later, in the throes of his successful television career, Matt admitted that he considers himself an agnostic. His reason: "I was very disturbed when Jesus found a demon in a guy and he put the demon into a herd of pigs, and then sent them off a cliff. What did the pigs do? I could never figure that out. It just seemed very unchristian. Technically, I'm an agnostic, but I definitely believe in hell—especially after watching the fall TV schedule."

Matt had a very typical childhood, but, he said ". . . the only difference is I took notes and vowed never to forget what it was like." Matt's childhood closely mirrored that of *The Simpsons* in one regard: the bickering between siblings, which was quite real in his family. Matt's older brother, Mark, and sister, Patty, constantly picked on him—the middle child—while he harassed his two younger sisters, Lisa and Maggie, for good measure.

Many of Matt's childhood adventures were to the nearby Washington Park and Hoyt Arboretum on his route to school. As he recalled, "They closed the old zoo when I was 4 or 5, but they left the cages, and when I was little we'd sneak in behind the bars. I actually swam in the green water of the bear pool."

In 1959, at age five, Matt committed his most outlandish prank yet. During a visit to the closed zoo, he hopped on an

Matt Groening poses with yellow hands, characteristic of his most famous and popular creations, the Simpsons. © *Reed MIDEM.*

abandoned flatcar and rode the railway. After the police arrived, two officers chased him into the woods. He outran them and met up with his brother at the local archery range.

Like many kids his age, Matt grew up glued to the television set, claiming he "watched way too much TV." His father introduced him to a myriad of popular television shows. He was a big fan of *Leave It to Beaver*, *The Adventures of Ozzie and Harriet*, which inspired him in his creation of *The Simpsons*, and, to some extent, *Dennis the Menace*, a show he found disappointing and on which he later partially based the character of Bart Simpson. Unlike the cyclonic, freckle-faced little kid in creator Hank Ketcham's popular comic strip, the television version of Dennis was, as Matt described, a "very namby-pamby Jay North [the child actor who played him], who didn't really do anything bad at all."

Mondays through Fridays after school, Matt plopped in front of the family's television console to watch KGW-TV's *Heck Harper's Cartoon Corral*, starring Portland perennial parade favorite and local television institution Heck Harper. During each live broadcast, the amiable guitar-strumming, singing cowboy—whose real name was Hector Flateau—mixed stories, songs, and reruns of old cartoons, including Felix the Cat, Popeye, Mister Magoo, Rocky and Bullwinkle, and others. In closing, he crooned, "Sadly, now we bid adieu to all our barnyard friends . . . all say toodle-loo."

Developing what became a lifelong fascination with animation, Matt's favorite cartoons were the classics. He loved all the Warner Bros. cartoons—Bugs Bunny, Daffy Duck, Road Runner and Wile E. Coyote; screwball animator Tex Avery's Droopy; and Max and Dave Fleischer's Betty Boop and Popeye. By far, his biggest influence was Jay Ward's adult-written *Rocky and His Friends*, starring the high-flying Rocket J. Squirrel and his pal Bullwinkle the Moose. In Matt's opinion, the show was successful because of "great writing, great voices, and great music" and "the animation didn't matter."

Matt likewise loved the work of legendary animator Walt Disney. He watched practically every show his studio made. At age five, Matt fulfilled his dream of visiting Disneyland, in Anaheim, California. After his father drove him there in the family car, he became so obsessed with the famed Disney amusement park that he made many return trips.

Matt's father was a cartoonist himself since the late 1940s, so Matt was around the creative arts his entire young life. In his words, Homer was the "hippest dad" in the neighborhood. Because of his work as single-panel gag cartoonist in the 1950s, drawing cartoons for *Coronet* and popular hot rod magazines, Homer subscribed to a wide range of general-interest magazines. As a result, Matt enthusiastically pored over cartoons published in such publications as the *New Yorker* and *Punch* long before he could read or understand them. It was his job afterward to stack them neatly in the basement.

Matt's hard-working and creative father, who spoke German until Matt went to school, constantly challenged and prodded Matt and the rest of the Groening brood. For Christmas and his children's birthdays, he typically bought them stockpiles of colored pencils and sketch pads for gifts at J. K. Gill, a book and office supply store chain in the Pacific Northwest. Instead of reading children's books to them, he drew the beginnings of original stories on a sketch pad and had them finish the rest. With sketch pads always lying around the house, Matt took up doodling. Before long, he was drawing on a regular basis.

Matt often spent hours sitting and reading comics at the local drugstore at the bottom of the hill where he lived. His favorites were Walt Kelly's *Pogo*, George Herriman's *Krazy Kat*, and Al Capp's *Li'l Abner*. His brother Mark, who also collected comics as a kid, turned him on to the great comic books in the 1950s—*Little Lulu*, *Uncle Scrooge*, and EC Comics horror and science-fiction comics like *Tales from the Crypt*. He also was a huge fan of 1960s superhero comics—*Spider-Man*, *Fantastic Four*, and *The Incredible Hulk*—until he found the stories weak and the drawings so carefully done that they distracted him. "I started with 'Archies,' because those are the fastest," Matt recalled. "You could read 'Archie' in about five seconds."

Another childhood haunt Matt frequented was Stadium Fred Meyer, a one-stop retailer—part of the famous Fred Meyer chain of hypermarkets—on West Burnside Street in the Hollywood district. There, for inspiration, he devoured his favorite comics and the wildly satirical *MAD* magazine, drawing ideas from them because he "liked the art." Occasionally, he joined Mark and his buddies in a secret clubhouse in a small room above a garage down the street from their house. It became their makeshift comics reading room.

Matt, in his words, "warped" himself when he was six years old after reading *The Child from Five to Ten*. The book explained the different behavior of children month by month. As he later explained in an interview, "I knew what I was supposed to be doing, and the sex questions I was suppose to be asking . . . My parents read this book and they said, 'Y'know, you never acted like the book said.' That's because I read the book."

BLAZING HIS OWN TRAIL

As a child, Matt did not exhibit much interest in school. He was very much a nonconformist at heart. He found school, as he once noted, "a rigid, humorless and uncreative place," with too many arbitrarily assigned "petty" rules and a grading system that was "unfair."

While attending Ainsworth Elementary School, one of Portland's finest public schools, he quickly developed a reputation as a classroom cutup. His greatest thrill was telling a joke that made the whole classroom burst into laughter and made the teacher turn beet red. Consequently, he developed a reputation as a troublemaker for his disruptive behavior of doodling during class time. "I always drew little creatures when I was in grade school," he said, "but no one could tell what they were . . . So I started drawing rabbits. It was after many, many clumsy attempts to draw bats and when I started to give some of them long ears, they said, 'Oh! Yeah! A rabbit!'"

His earliest run-in happened in first grade, while standing with his classmates in a circle on the playground during recess. When his teacher, Mrs. Hoover, suddenly announced, "Quiet, children!" Matt, for no apparent reason other than perhaps youthful exuberance, let out a loud, high-pitched shriek. It was so loud Mrs. Hoover raised her voice and asked, "Who blew that whistle?"

Matt instantly clammed up. He knew he was in trouble. To the sheer bemusement of his classmates, Mrs. Hoover went crazy searching every one of them for a whistle, but she never found one. Despite the lack of physical evidence, she pinned Matt as the source of the commotion. She promptly took him up to the principal's office. It was one incident he never forgot—his first run-in with authority and stifling of creative expression. "The rest of my life," he reflected, "has been blowing invisible whistles and making people wonder."

On other occasions, he ceaselessly doodled instead of focusing on his class work. So his teachers confiscated his crude drawings and ripped them into shreds. "I couldn't understand why stuff that brought me such joy could annoy so many teachers," he once said. After Matt mouthed off, his teachers either sent him to sit in the corner of the classroom in front of his classmates or to cool his heels in the principal's office. He often thought to himself, "I don't know how I'm gonna do it, but somehow I'm gonna make this wasted time pay off."

After getting into trouble a few times, Matt learned a few new tricks that only worsened his situation: "I took a bit of string and learned how to make a hangman's noose, which got me into further trouble, and sent me to the corner again. Then I learned to blow bubbles off the end of my tongue, a skill which I tormented my sisters with again and again" Periodically, he made high-pitched "meowing noises" that also drove his teachers insane.

In sixth grade, Matt was ushered back into the principal's office—again. This time it was for tossing an encyclopedia out of a second-story window. "I could understand getting sent to the principal's office for dropping an encyclopedia out the window," he later told a reporter, "but I couldn't understand them ripping my cartoons up."

By age nine, Matt became adept creatively. He credits his development to starting a group he called the Creature Club, an "exclusive" neighborhood organization—whose motto was "I'm peculiar"—that met in an abandoned haunted house not far from his home. Their main activity was spending long hours drawing scary monsters, building haunted houses, and dreaming up complex fantasies, like an imaginary civilization of bugs, called Slugonia. During these artistic pursuits, they all tried drawing the famed comic-book caped crusader Batman. After his did not turn out so well, Matt concluded he could never draw muscles realistically. So he used animals instead of "muscle guys" to draw his first comic strip, *Tales of the Enchanted Forest*. It included a villain called Rotten Rabbit. A much cruder and formative version of his later *Life in Hell* cartoon rabbit, Binky, Rotten Rabbit was, as Matt remembered, "the only character people could recognize . . . I had an owl and people thought it was a little bear."

In fifth grade in 1964, Matt developed two new characters, unaware of their future importance: Akbar and Jeff, whom he later popularized in his syndicated alternative comic strip, *Life in Hell*. Garbed in Charlie Brown zigzag T-shirts, the pair evolved from Matt's failed attempt to draw Charles M. Schulz's Charlie Brown character. Schulz, as well as

Dr. Seuss, was among Matt's childhood influences. Matt named Jeff after his best friend in grade school and Akbar after an old king in India.

In the 1960s, Matt's father entered a creative period. A self-taught filmmaker, he wrote, produced, directed, and edited various industrial films for clients. He had formed his own agency in 1958. He also made a string of unusual water-related seven-minute color short films, including *Get Wet*, *Getting Wetter*, *Psychedelic Wet*, and *Study in Wet*, and won many awards for his work. Later he directed a number of promotional trailers, including the trailer for the 1969 Tony Curtis comedy feature, *Those Daring Young Men in Their Jaunty Jalopies*. Homer passed down his love of filmmaking to Matt. He taught him film editing at an early age.

One of Matt's many pleasures was going to the movies. He and his closest childhood friends, Eric, Tim, and Duncan Smith, sons of a renowned children's doctor, Lendon Smith, used to sneak into big downtown movie theaters, like the Paramount and Orpheum, which Matt called "the easy ones." In the late 1950s, he became upset after he saw a rereleased screening of Walt Disney's *Bambi* (1942). Parking himself up in the balcony of the Paramount Theater, he became so frightened by the film's realism during the dramatic scene in which Bambi awakens to the forest ablaze and tries escaping the fiery inferno that he began sobbing. His sister Patty finally had to carry him to the mezzanine section of the theater to settle him down.

Three years later, Mark forever scandalized him after taking him to his first movie with "hell" in the title. Instead of his first choice, George Pal's Oscar-winning musical adventure, *Tom Thumb*, he took him to see *Hell Drivers* (1957), about an ex-con truck driver who exposes corruption in his company. It was playing on a double bill at the Orpheum Theater with *Sergeants 3* (1962), starring the so-called "Rat Pack"—Frank Sinatra, Dean Martin, Sammy Davis Jr., and Joey Bishop—in a boozy comedy-western that, in his words, "bewildered me." Another flick that tormented Matt was William Cameron Menzie's original science-fiction movie, *Invaders from Mars* (1953), in which a frightened young boy suspects aliens are taking control of humans after implanting a controlling device at the base of their necks that dramatically alters their personality. The film's cheesy, but then-believable, special effects

Matt's father, cartoonist, ad man, and filmmaker extraordinaire Homer Groening, pictured in 1973, was a major creative influence early in his life. (*Courtesy:* The Oregonian.)

included stiff-walking, bazooka-blasting, pajama-costumed aliens and an eerie tentacle-headed Martian chief in a glass bubble. Despite the film's second-rate cast, its scary images left Matt paralyzed with fear and dominated his dreams for days.

As a kid, Matt splurged on watching many other low-brow classics on Portland's KPTV Channel 12. These included the *Joe E. Brown Theater*, a weekend showcase of the giant-mouthed comedian's strangely mirthless movies, and reruns of bottom-of-the-barrel movie serials airing right before it, among them Universal Pictures' 12-chapter serial *The Phantom Creeps* (1939).

BREAKING THE CREATIVE MOLD

Meanwhile, Matt's pursuit of creative self-expression showed considerable promise in another area: as a writer. He loved dreaming up ideas and putting them down on paper—poems, limericks, stories, and comic books. He realized then, as he said, that "this was what I was going to be doing for the rest of my life." He was not so certain that he would make a living in the creative arts, but expected he would "always be doing some form of child's play" as he grew older.

Matt's hellish imagination jelled at a very early age. In 1962, when he was in third grade, the eight-year-old's writing was published in his first national publication. A popular children's magazine, *Jack and Jill*, ran a national short-story contest inviting young readers to submit their original endings to a Halloween story published in the magazine. It was about a boy named Little Davy who goes up into the attic and after pretending to be a ghost and bumping his head, decides he knows what he wants to be for Halloween. Matt submitted his entry among hundreds of others. To his credit, he won for his morbid finale, which was published in a later issue.

"In everybody else's story, Davy said, 'Oh, I wanna be a cowboy, oh, I wanna be a fireman.' and so on," Matt commented. "But in my story, the kid bumped his head, and he died. He got killed on the spot. And the family felt so bad they boarded up the attic. They boarded up the door and nailed it shut. And every year on that day the little boy would float down the stairs, his ghostly image would eat dinner in silence, and he would return."

For his prize, Matt won a trip to attend the broadcast of the local Portland version of the syndicated children's series *Romper Room*. The weekday show featured games, exercises, songs, and moral lessons for preschool-aged viewers. The experience was totally humiliating. On live television, the bright-eyed and perky host stuck a microphone in Matt's face, asking him to respond to something. In a Homer Simpson-like moment, all Matt could say was, "I don't know what to say. I don't know what to say." He was so embarrassed he said not another word on the show. It ranked as one of the low points of his young life.

Possessing such a wild imagination, Matt envisioned starring in his own show. In fact, he recorded on an audio tape recorder his own imaginary program, *The Matt Groening Show*, complete with its own Matt Groening Orchestra and catchy theme song that he wrote and performed himself. It went something like this: "First you hear a mighty cheer, then you know that Groening's here. Then a streak of color flashes on the ground. You know it's not a train or a comet or a plane. You know it must be Matt Groening, cool guy. Matt Groening, Matt Groening, Matt Groening. Not a coward, super-powered Matt Groening, coolest guy there is in town, coolest guy around."

After singing the song for his classmates, many made fun of him and his loopy theme. As he remembered, girls did not get it but boys thought it was way "too cool."

By 1966, then 12, Matt's contempt for school remained largely unchanged. Now calling Ainsworth Elementary an "oppressive, stifling place," his extracurricular activities that deviated from instruction at hand were still frowned upon. That year, displaying a strong sense of drama and self-pity, he started keeping a diary of his so-called "crimes and punishments." As an unruly sixth grader sitting outside the principal's office, he scribbled daily entries into his tiny green spiral notebook:

APRIL 6: 7 people got in trouble today, including me.
APRIL 22: People got in trouble 26 times today.
MAY 3: I have to write, 'I must remember to be quiet in class,'
    500 times and turn it in tomorrow.

> MAY 7: I'm making a graph of how many times people get in trouble in class.

Matt became so afraid to go to school that Homer gave him "pep talks" while driving him up Vista Avenue to school every morning and dropping him off. "Remember," he would say, "you're a good boy."

Unfortunately, Matt's teachers saw a much different version of the prepubescent teen Homer knew and loved. Young, bored, and restless, Matt either daydreamed by drawing cartoons or reading escapist literature like books on World War II while fantasizing about his plans of escape from the "prison camp" school. Unknowingly, his inspired doodlings became a more entertaining version of himself and of the arrogance and hypocrisy of his experiences and what, as he said, "I would like to see when I was a kid."

Nurturing his antiestablishment views, the disgruntled teen regularly visited the local "hippie" record shop, Longhair Music, on Southwest Park Avenue in downtown Portland. The store was the largest carrier in the area of underground comics by alternative cartoonists, many of which were intended for adult audiences. One artist whose work he grew to admire was the revolutionary cartoonist Robert Crumb, creator of *Fritz the Cat* and *Mr. Natural*, along with Gilbert Shelton's the *Fabulous Furry Freak Brothers*, and one of the best-known underground comics in the late 1960s, *Zap Comix*, featuring the work of popular counterculture cartoonists of the day.

Fanning his tastes of the bizarre, Matt likewise developed an insatiable appetite for popular underground cinema. On weekends, he took in showings of films like Andy Warhol's *Tarzan and Jane Regained . . . Sort of* (1964), Red Grooms's *Fat Feet* (1966), and George Kuchar's *Hold Me While I'm Naked* (1966) at Portland State University (formerly called Portland State College) on SW Broadway. He even cut out of school early one day to see the noon screening of Richard Lester's strangely humorous antiwar farce, *How I Won the War* (1967).

By 1968, during eighth grade, Matt's relationship with the school's principal reached a crescendo. Tired of his brooding, disruptive behavior, the principal told Matt's parents during a parent conference as nice and friendly as possible that the best thing that could happen was for Matt "to graduate."

Fortunately, for everyone's sake, Matt did. In the fall of 1969, shunning the radical Adams High School, he attended Lincoln High School in downtown Portland, where eventually he hit his stride. Scared and self-conscious at first in his new environment, the gawky freshman overcame his social paralysis after realizing he was no different from anyone else. He quickly learned "You are what you are," despite school.

Emerging from his shell, Matt formed many lasting friendships that extended beyond his family and his Lincoln High days. The funny and extroverted teen became involved with those sharing similar passions—writing stories, drawing cartoons, and making movies (some of whom later pursued creative careers of their own), including James K. Angell III, Richard Gehr, Dan Avshalomov, Lawrence Shlim, and Dan Helms.

Even then, Matt exhibited a darkly humorous style. One time while visiting Matt's basement bedroom, Helms eyed a big smiley-face poster on the wall with a semicircle drawn between the eyes. He asked, "What's that semicircle?"

Matt shrugged and said, "Brain tumor."

Matt displayed similar comic sensibilities when he and Gehr, who went on to become a successful rock critic for the alternative tabloid *The Village Voice*, worked part-time in the kitchen at the Kearney Care Center, a nearby convalescent home. Matt's motto for the place was, "You can eat what you choose, but you can't chew what you eat."

CREATING HIS UNDERGROUND COMIC STYLE

Not surprisingly, Matt wrote and cartooned for the school newspaper, *The Cardinal Times*. He published an underground newspaper, called *Bilge Rat*, and cocreated with a high school pal, Angell, the cartoon character Ace Noodleman, and their own Lincoln High board game. He also outraged teachers after entering pages he termed "gibberish" for a school poetry contest that serious judges were forced to read out loud.

With comics playing a major part of his childhood, Matt and his friends formed the Komix Appreciation Club. A half-dozen of them met during lunch period in the library to practice their cartoons, many in the same cryptic style, as Matt became like a mentor to them. As Helms related, "It was pretty generous of him to give me that kind of encouragement."

On campus, Matt enjoyed numerous other pursuits. He supported the student-run Film Group, producing with his friends their own home-made films, individually or collectively. Their early cinematic treasures included *Salmon Street Saga, Lightning Tour of Lincoln* (a minute-long race through school halls), and *Drugs: Killers or Dillers?*, featuring a crazed clown with an eggbeater, inspired by angry villagers carrying torches and pitchforks in old monster movies.

Matt and his friends also created their own social entity, The Banana Gang, an imaginary group of "greaser thugs . . . blamed for all sorts of goofy deeds around the school, such as smearing locker locks with bananas." Later, when invited to a party at the Smith brothers' home, they came in costume as Banana Gang greasers. They had a promotional picture snapped, intended to be used to promote their film *Salmon Street Saga*, which ended up in the high school's 1971 yearbook in their junior year.

Back then Matt was not "a slave to convention," as he once said. He created his own and experienced other achievements, like starring in the school's comedy stage production of *Send Me No Flowers*, based on the 1960 Broadway play.

Bookending his interest in cartooning and amateur filmmaking was Matt's developing passion for music. His favorite band was Captain Beefheart (alias Don Von Vliet) and the Magic Band, a group that came onto the scene in 1965 and mixed rock, blues, and psychedelia with free jazz, avant-garde, and contemporary experimental composition. Matt saved his lunch money to buy their 1969 double-album, *Trout Mask Replica*, produced by his all-time musical hero, Frank Zappa, to add to his small collection of LPs. Listening to the album the first time, he thought, "They're not even trying. This is just a bunch of meaningless, psychedelic nonsense and sloppy music." By the fifth or sixth replaying, however, he understood what they were striving for, noting, "This is great. This is the greatest album I've ever heard."

Matt's appreciation for the iconoclastic group spilled over into gym class. When he and Gehr used to run "punishment laps" ordered by their instructor, they broke into singing song lyrics from *Trout Mask Replica*, and crowed enthusiastically, "This is the greatest album of 1984," inferring that "If this is how great pop music is in 1969, just think how great it's going to be in the future."

In high school, Matt showed flashes of his staunch antiauthority views and liberal political leanings as well. In jest with his fellow Lincoln High misfits, he created a sarcastic political faction of his own: Teens of Decency, whose slogan was: "If you're against decency, what are you for?" Running as the group's candidate, he was elected student body president on the simple promise of ridding halls of "teacher patrols." After school, he hung around with antiwar students from a nearby college.

Before graduating in 1972, Matt applied at only two colleges: far-off Harvard University (he was not accepted) and The Evergreen State College, a small four-year, progressive liberal arts and sciences college in Olympia, Washington. The school had become a haven for hippies and poets and revolutionaries in the Pacific Northwest. After the state legislator had railed against the ultra-liberal university, "I decided at that point," Matt explained, "if a right-wing Republican was against it, I was for it."

That fall, Matt started his pursuit of higher learning at this so-called "rebellious outpost," known for, as he remembered, "no grades, no tests, no classes [they were called 'seminars'], no football team, and no jobs once you graduate." He responded to his newfound freedom by studying journalism, philosophy, filmmaking, and popular culture, with a burst of self-discipline. Believing his talent was more as a writer than a cartoonist, he wanted to become a famous journalist and served as editor of the school's paper, the *Cooper Point Journal* (almost named the *Mud Bay Journal*). His original ambition was to become a writer for the *Oregonian* newspaper after the paper's film critic Ted Mahar gave a talk at high school that inspired him.

As editor, Matt turned the school paper into, as one fellow classmate called it, a "muckraking scandal sheet" that routinely attacked the state legislature and public figures and started to look like the *National Enquirer*. Consequently, the paper divided the university into two camps: people who made signs and marched on campus and people who laughed so hard they threw up. Matt was proud enough of his work that he sent copies of the paper to an editor of the *Oregonian*, who was largely unimpressed. He replied that Matt would "never get a job in journalism."

During his time on the school paper, Matt met three other like-minded budding cartoonists with whom he spent much of his time in the campus newspaper office trading ideas, dreams, and good-natured insults: the redheaded dynamo, Lynda Barry; the visionary cartoonist, Charlie Burns; and the self-described local hick who drew only for laughs, Steve Willis. A decade later, all four would become household names for their cartooning.

Barry, who studied at Evergreen and was trained as a painter, remembers fondly her times at The Evergreen State College, especially Matt when he was on deadline as the editor of the paper. "He'd take this piece of paper and wire and wrap it around his head so that there was an antenna sticking up," she recalled, "which was his signal that he didn't want to be disturbed."

Matt befriended Lynda after learning she had written a fan letter to one of Matt's favorite writers, Joseph Heller, author of the influential novel *Catch-22* (1961), and that the famed author actually wrote her back. Calling her one of "my most important influences," Matt published several of her cartoons in the school's paper. Inspired, he decided to turn to cartooning to see if he could do something "a little bit different."

Up until then, underground comics had become a popular art form, but the market for them was virtually dead by the time he attended Evergreen, until a new breed of cartoonists made their mark. Matt noticed how Lynda's cartoons were wild and funny, but with a very strong point of view. "I had been trying to make other people laugh, and I found out by looking at Lynda's cartoons that if you make yourself laugh," he explained, "it's generally good for other people as well . . . She taught me that you could do a cartoon on whatever struck your fancy."

Following her example, Matt published his own cartoons in the *Cooper Point Journal*. They were drawn in his usual gonzo cartoon style, sketchy figures with lots of text. Reaction to his and Lynda's published cartoons from students and their peers, mostly "humorless hippies," as he described them, were both positive and negative. They showed indifference to their jokes, saying, "You think you're better than us?" Topics such as race and sex were taboo. In the skewed world of Matt's critics at the time, to laugh at such humor meant somebody was being oppressed, with the humorist or cartoonist viewed as the ultimate oppressor. As Matt related, "We had people who lived in teepees and they were angry at people who lived in wooden structures."

As a cartoonist, Matt was largely influenced by Jack Hamm's clearly written, step-by-step handbook, *Cartooning the Head & Figure*. This so-called bible for animators covered how to evoke a range of emotions with the crudest little ink squiggles and through different styles, positions, and variations of caricaturing and cartooning that emphasized humor and exaggeration. In drawing cartoons for the paper, Matt experimented with using more sophisticated drawing techniques, but those who saw his work flatly told him, "Look at Thurber, go his way. You can't draw." (James Thurber, who drew in a very simple style, was a popular American author and cartoonist best known for witty cartoons and short stories.) In fact, the more he tried to improve his drawings, the worse they looked. Matt admitted to doing "really sloppy stuff" before later tightening up his drawing style.

Under Evergreen's progressive style of learning, students took one subject each semester, with classes that lasted as long as six hours a day. Matt chose to study with "the toughest teacher on campus," philosophy professor Mark Levensky. He became a seminal figure in Matt's life. During their last class meeting just before he graduated, the professor told him, "This is what you do tolerably well. Now you have to ask yourself: Is it worth doing?"

Riddled with doubt and without ever answering the question, Matt eventually found his groove. In his heart, he was determined to become a writer. Little did Matt realize just how difficult fulfilling his dream would become.

Life in Hell

After graduating from college, Matt, now a 23-year-old wannabe writer, eagerly set out to prove himself. In August 1977, with his philosophy diploma in hand, he left the clean and green Pacific Northwest to move to Los Angeles because that was where, as he once stated, "the action was" to land a "dream" writing job. He drove there in a 1972 lime-green Datsun sedan his parents had given him. As he later declared, "I wanted to be a writer and it seemed to be the place where writing was the most overpaid." One of his inspirations for moving there was his idol, rocker Frank Zappa, whose music he grew up listening to, and he thought if "LA was good enough for him, I should check it out."

Matt's first day in Los Angeles was memorable, to say the least. Arriving at midnight on one of the hottest days that summer, his first taste of the city was listening to a drunken radio disc-jockey—fired the next day for his inebriated behavior—decrying how it was "100 degrees outside." After entering the city, his sedan broke down, twice. The first breakdown happened while he was driving in the fast lane of the Hollywood Freeway, which crisscrosses through Los Angeles. As impatient drivers passed him, he was left stranded until he restarted his car. The second breakdown came while he was traveling on Sunset Boulevard near the high-rent district of Beverly Hills, where some of the area's well-to-do honked loudly as they sped their high-priced, fancy cars around him.

Matt moved to Los Angeles on the pretense of working as a journalist for the *Los Angeles Free Press*, a local alternative paper at the time. But the day he walked into the office, the receptionist, who greeted him, was crying uncontrollably and said to him, "Don't work for those bastards." Consequently, he never worked for the paper.

Frustrated, broke, and without a job, Matt's start in Los Angeles was nothing like he had dreamed. During the next two years, he did everything in his power to forge a career as a writer. He accepted a series of demoralizing or "hellish" jobs to make ends meet. That August, the very first job he landed shortly after taking the receptionist's advice was as a movie extra in the 1978 NBC made-for-TV movie *When Every Day Was the Fourth of July*. The movie was shot on location in San Pedro in the heat of the summer. Matt, dressed in a wool suit three sizes too small, played a member of a lynch mob in a scene where a member gets into a fight with a vendor selling miniature electric chairs. Filming lasted into the late-night hours. At midnight, Matt finally quit. Retrieving his street clothes, he hitchhiked his way back to Los Angeles that night.

Working every menial job in the meantime—as a busboy, a dishwasher at a nursing home, a landscaper at a local sewage treatment plant, and as a clerk at a photocopying store—Matt's plan was still to become writer, even though he admittedly had no idea of how to make that a reality.

Looking through "Help Wanted" ads, Matt came across one listing in the *Los Angeles Times* that read: "Wanted: Writer/Chauffeur." Figuring this was one way to get into the business, he quickly answered the ad and was hired. His duties were to chauffeur around an eccentric, retired, 88-year-old Western movie director by day and listen to him regale with stories of his prolific life. Then, at night, Matt was to ghostwrite his memoirs, with another person employed to type up stories from the day before. Previous writers/chauffeurs had tried unsuccessfully to work with the idiosyncratic director on his unpublished tome that had topped 1,000 pages by the time Matt arrived.

Matt described his workday this way: "During the day, while I drove him around, he would point out the sights and explain to me about his life. Unfortunately, he was going senile. So one day we would drive up to the canyon and he'd point at a mansion and say, 'That is where Cary Grant used to live. I'll never forget the parties there,' and he'd tell me some story about Greta Garbo and Jimmy Stewart and whoever. We'd drive by the same mansion the next day and he'd go, 'Ah, look, Laurel and Hardy's house.' So not only did Cary Grant's house turn into Laurel and Hardy's house, but he somehow had it in his mind that Laurel and Hardy lived *together*."

One hang-up in working with him, Matt felt, was the aging helmsman was "totally obsessed" with his mother who had lived with him until she reached the ripe old age of 105, and every single part of the book was about *her*. For example, in one passage, as Matt related, he wrote: "Today I met Cecil B. DeMille. I ran home immediately to tell mother."

Matt lasted only for a few months. The doddering director finally fired him over the "quality" of his writing.

After his dismissal, Matt scrambled for work. He applied for a job at *TV Guide* to write synopses of shows. He was told he did not get the job because he used the word "lesbian" in his description of what a show was about in his writing sample.

The horrors of living in Los Angeles beat Matt down. In fact, he hated it. He was surprised by the crowded freeways, sludge brown air, and brusque denizens. At times he yearned for the clean blue sky, green surroundings, and friendly people of his native Pacific Northwest. At one point, his girlfriend broke up with him, his car blew up, and he was out of work again. To make matters worse, he could not pay the rent for his apartment. He was living in a place where the tenant immediately below him played rockabilly music full blast at three in the morning. Annoyed by the man's hellish behavior, Matt retaliated by placing the speakers to his stereo facedown and blasting what he called his "superior reggae" music right back at him. The guy continued his annoying habit until Matt finally took a cinder block that held up his makeshift bookshelf, raised it up high, and dropped it full force on the floor, knocking the light fixture out of the guy's ceiling.

TURNING HIS MISERY INTO AN ART FORM

Miserable, Matt came to the grim reality that living in Los Angeles was, in his words, "hell." While his experience was not unique, this sudden realization marked the dawning of a new idea and new direction that started as a hobby. That first year, Matt did not wallow in self-pity or lean on his family and relatives about his plight. Instead he did what he always did as a child: He started drawing. Inspired by the ugliness around him, he feverishly began doodling crudely drawn cartoons in a newsletter form. He recorded on paper his observations about Los Angeles and his dreary life in the mold of the great alternative comic artists he admired as a kid and mailed them to his friends back home. Originally drawing them to amuse himself, his cartoons became the seed of his darkly funny, autobiographical comic strip *Life in Hell*, which launched his career as a professional cartoonist. He loosely titled the strip after a chapter he remembered reading in renowned German-American philosopher, poet, and academic scholar Walter Kaufman's 1958 book, *Critique of Religion and Philosophy*, entitled, "How to Go to Hell."

From the outset, *Life in Hell* chronicled the teeth-gritting frustrations, indignities, and heartbreaks of life through the eyes of Matt's bucktoothed, bug-eyed, and chronically embittered alter-ego, Binky the rabbit. Once describing him as "a stand-in for me ranting about what annoyed me," he named him long before reading underground cartoonist Justin Green's masterpiece comic book, *Binky Brown Meets the Holy Virgin Mary*. The supporting cast he developed was limited to Binky's perpetually irritable feminist girlfriend, Sheba. Some have incorrectly insisted that Matt modeled Binky after his own neurotic behavior; actually, his real-life inspiration was a character from his college dorm with, as Matt stated, "large eyes, big front teeth, and romantic difficulties." While Matt's romantic encounters back in college were tragic, his dorm mates, in his opinion, were, truly "comical."

Matt never created the strip for the purpose of commercialization. In fact, his format was inconsistent. It eschewed the usual commercial niceties of using the same format each time—sometimes appearing as a big, one-panel cartoon, other times with smaller panels tucked in among a mass of words. In the beginning, Binky's hostile ranting and raving in each strip was based on Matt's heartfelt feelings about many issues he was facing in his personal life. His earliest versions were, as he noted, "a lot more bitter." As the strip evolved, drawing it was like "playing to me." However, after a few months, he overhauled Binky. He made him less an angst-ridden complainer, and more a victim of an aggressor instead. "The second I made the rabbit a victim," he admitted, "people started liking the comic strip. The more tragedies that befell this poor little rodent, the more positive the response I got."

During the heyday of punk rock, Matt landed a job as a clerk at the very hip Licorice Pizza record store on Sunset Strip, right across from the Whisky a Go-Go, a famous and popular nightclub that featured fringed-dressed go-go girl dancers in white boots. Licorice Pizza's gimmick was giving "free licorice" to its customers, including a number of unsavory-looking homeless people. Selling records, psychedelia, punks, and even backdoor drug paraphernalia to rock stars of the day, the store attracted an eclectic clientele.

While working there, Matt photocopied his fledgling *Life in Hell* strips on legal paper. Then he stapled and self-published them as an ongoing comic book series featuring his black-and-white, line-drawn Binky the rabbit. He later admitted he would have added color if he could draw the characters fast, but keeping his drawing style simple allowed him to hurry and move on to the next idea. He sent the first issue to 20 friends back in the Northwest. They thought it was "pretty damn funny" and encouraged him to do more. He sold them as well in the punk music corner of the store, where they were displayed with records of punk groups like X, the Deadbeats, and the Germs, and punk fanzines like *Slash*, *Flipside*, and *Starting Fires*. He sold many copies; by his sixth issue, he printed as many as 500 copies. Punk patrons at the store who bought the booklets either liked them or tore them up, which, as Matt joked in a *Newsweek* interview, "could have meant they liked it, too."

In 1978, Matt made his first professional sale of the strip to the publisher of the ultra-trendy and glossy *WET* magazine, launched two years earlier by Venice, California-based architecture graduate Leonard Koren as "The Magazine of Gourmet Bathing." After its first few issues, he expanded its scope and design to feature graphically innovative color covers and stories on art, music, and fashion, including the 1970s Venice culture, the Los Angeles punk rock scene, and the California hippie movement. Matt's first *Life in Hell* strip, called "Forbidden Words," was published in its September/October 1978 issue.

Late that fall, after publishing six issues of his homemade comic book that ranged from 8 to 56 pages in length, Matt marched into the offices of two new Los Angeles alternative weeklies seeking work: the tabloid-size *LA Weekly* and its cross-town competitor the *Los Angeles Reader*, a spin-off of the *Chicago Reader*. He was quickly hired by the *LA Weekly* but stayed on only for one week.

Between November and December, shortly after the *Los Angeles Reader's* launch, Matt met with its founding editor James Vowell and pitched an idea for a cover story about "artists who painted the fancy billboards" on Hollywood's world-famous Sunset Boulevard. After giving him the go-ahead to write the piece, Vowell published it as the paper's main cover story in its early February 1979 edition. At least that's how Vowell remembers it. Matt recalls the events of his hiring differently. He routinely says in his interviews that after showing Vowell his "little strips," he hired him "on the spot."

Either way, for the next few months into early spring, Matt worked under Vowell and the paper's original publisher, Jane Levine, doing everything he could to help the publication succeed. Levine finally offered him the job of operations manager, responsible for the paper's distribution. The fledgling weekly developed a large readership for its lengthy, thoughtful reviews of concerts, plays, and movies in the surrounding Los Angeles area. Matt's route distributing the paper stretched from the inland city of Glendale to the coastal community of Malibu, delivering 60,000 papers every Friday, up from 28,000 per week at the

Sitting behind his drawing table in his creative garage-studio lair, dubbed the "Bat Cave," in Venice Beach, California, Matt prepares to draw a panel for his widely syndicated strip that started it all, *Life in Hell*. *(Courtesy: Los Angeles Times Photographic Archive, UCLA Library.)* © *Los Angeles Times.*

time he was promoted. One of Matt's main objectives, he claims, in delivering to Malibu was its close proximity to the Pacific Ocean, so he could "go swimming."

As one of only three original staff members, including Levine, Vowell, and himself, Matt helped out in other areas—answering phones, doing typesetting and pasteup, and editing, everything except selling advertisements. On the side, he kept peddling his *Life in Hell* strip in hopes of convincing Vowell to publish his cartoons. As Vowell remembers, "We would go over to the typesetter in Hollywood every Monday and Tuesday night. We often took breaks for dinner and Matt would draw sketches of cartoon characters on napkins and hand them to me. I would critique his sketches, saying things like 'lips are too big, Matt.'"

A few months later, Levine appointed Matt to assistant editor, to work directly under Vowell. While writing feature articles, editing stories, and compiling weekly entertainment and music listings, Matt persistently showed his boss his cartoon ideas. (That year, Matt formed an umbrella company for his cartooning, Matt Groening Productions, serving as its president.) Finally, in April 1980, Vowell invited him to draw his strip for the back pages of the *Reader*. He published his first *Life in Hell* cartoon in its Friday, April 25th edition. As Matt, a self-admitted liberal, joked in 1988, "My strip started when Reagan was running for president in 1980, so 'Life in Hell' was an appropriate title. I swore that if George Bush [George W. Bush's father] lost [when he ran for president], I was going to change the name of the strip to 'Life Is Swell.'"

Thereafter, revered for its subtle blend of the lighter and darker sides of the human psyche and for entertaining and amusing its readers with its personal and universal human truths, *Life in Hell* became a popular weekly fixture. As Matt confessed back then, "I didn't expect there to be an audience for what I was drawing because I didn't see anything drawn that crummy. There was noting else as crude, but obviously having a forum every week was very motivating to develop more stuff."

CONQUERING CARTOONING AND MUSIC

Proving his value to the paper in a short time, Matt fulfilled two passions at once—cartooning and music. By 1982, Vowell assigned Matt to write his own weekly rock music column—or music "gossip" column—called "Sound Mix." His musical tastes, however, as he has confessed, are "so obnoxious I can't play my records for anyone else. I just sit by myself and play them because they would drive everyone else away." With a broad range of favorites like Frank Zappa, Captain Beefheart, Yma Sumac, Dimanda Galas, easygoing music of the 1960s, and Indian music, as he later stated, "My taste got so eccentric that I was no longer able to sell any articles."

Upgrading to a 1962 Ford Fairlane with a then state-of-the-art push-button transmission, Matt looked and acted the part of an underground newspaper critic. He sported glasses, hip facial stubble, and a self-proclaimed "bad" haircut with, as he noted, "the vague sensation that my career choice was ridiculous and, of course, the empty wallet, you know, writing for alternative newsweeklies." For his column, he wrote about mostly local bands and groups, like Severed Head in a Bag, which played in basement nightclubs. One night, while driving to a show to cover for his next column, his car broke down. Instead of reviewing that evening's musical group, he wrote about the adventure of his car breaking down. According to Matt, "people liked that stuff as much as the prose about music." Afterward, he started writing each week about his humorous misadventures—how his girlfriend would not come to visit him because "her car kept getting robbed"—and *rarely* about music. Instead he talked about his life and childhood, describing "various enthusiasms, obsessions, pet peeves, and problems" he experienced. "I think the people who ran the 'Reader' felt so guilty about how little they were paying people," he explained, "that they let them write about whatever they wanted."

Perhaps that was the case early on, but to add more music to his column, Matt made stuff up and wrote reviews of nonexistent and fictional bands and records. Such flat-out fabrications, however, did not sit well with Levine, Vowell, or the paper's most devoted readers. In a follow-up column, he openly confessed to taking such creative license in some cases, but swore everything else in his column was absolutely true.

After the fact, Matt reviewed legitimate artists, mostly obscure rock bands. In one review, he viciously panned then Oingo Boingo lead singer/songwriter Danny Elfman, who responded with an irate letter to the editor. Later, Elfman went on to become a successful composer of film and television scores and wrote the theme for *The Simpsons*. When Matt started producing *The Simpsons* and had his first meeting with Elfman to explore having him score the theme, he hoped he would not remember the incident, but he did. As Matt remarked, "He also forgave me because I had done a number of comic strips that skewered rock critics the way he thought they should be skewered."

Now and then, Matt also actually interviewed rock stars for his column. He once sat down to do a one-on-one interview with Grammy award-winning rocker David Byrne, the Scottish-born musician who cofounded the American new wave band Talking Heads. During his interview, he asked a series of relevant questions in order to write a lengthy column about Byrne and the band. In the course of their conversation, he was horrified when the tape in his recorder suddenly broke and hopelessly started spinning around unattended. "I'd never seen a tape break," Matt said an in interview. "It had broken at the very beginning!"

Giving the young, stubble-faced columnist a long, hard stare, the dark-haired, thick-lashed bass guitarist band member said, "I hope you have a good memory!"

Embarrassed, Matt finished up. Afterward, like "a teenager recreating a conversation," as Matt put it, he did his best to recall the conversation, splitting hairs throughout his article and hoping readers would never know the difference. He fleshed out the piece with unremarkable phrases, writing, "and then he went" and "and then I went." He even spun part of their conversation this way:

"Then he goes, 'So I'm the Talking Heads.'"

"And I go, 'So, are they a good group?'"

"And he goes, 'Yeah!'"

In spite of his concerted efforts to improve his column, Vowell asked Matt to give up doing his music column and suggested he write a humor column under a different title instead. His new columns were like illustrated essays covering a wide assortment of cultural topics, one of them being "Sixteen Types of Sisters," in his usual inimitable style.

Paid meagerly for his work, Matt struggled like most artists to make it in a town where many dreamed big and many more failed. In the early 1980s, he lived in a roach-infested, Hollywood apartment not far from Paramount Studios. He was so poor that he rounded up any loose change he could find under chair cushions just to buy a hamburger at his favorite haunt, Astro Burger, on Melrose Avenue, right across from the studio. As his longtime friend Gary Panter, who later made his mark with his wildly creative set designers as a codesigner of CBS's *Pee-Wee's Playhouse*, recalled, "Matt's place was totally trashed, and the floor was covered with change—either he just threw it there or it fell out of his pockets. He lived like that because all of his attention was focused on his ideas."

A great communicator despite his struggles, Matt could be very persuasive. He got together with Panter to go places or just to talk. Plotting and scheming on how they were going to invade the media, they often sat around fantasizing about how they were going to get rich. Sometimes they would ask, "If or when we make our big mark in the world, are we going to live the way millionaires do on *Lifestyles of the Rich and Famous,* or are we going to live the way we do now—except with a lot more comic books, magazines and records lying around?"

It was not long before Matt found the former to be true in his case.

3

Hell Is Not So Bad

Always thinking of himself as a writer first, Matt was definitely living the make-or-break life of a cartoonist. Despite later calling his cartooning career a "fluke," this unredeemed doodler-turned comic-strip cartoonist's work was so uniquely different from most comic strips that it was only a matter of time before it became immensely popular and he enjoyed the sweet taste of success.

In drawing his strip, Matt spent a couple of hours each week at the drawing board, usually drawing his strip beginning at midnight every Tuesday, just a few hours before his deadline. The rest of the time he routinely carried notebooks of ideas around for future strips. Though vowing many times to finish his strips ahead of schedule, he found he worked better under the gun. Drawing them was personally the hardest part for Matt, something he attributed to what he called a "very low attention span" on his part.

As his strip became widely published, Matt added additional supporting characters. In 1983, he introduced Binky's neurotic, illegitimate, one-eared son, Bongo, brought into the world after a single night of passion with a near-perfect stranger five years earlier and who unexpectedly dropped Bongo on Binky's doorstep. In subsequent appearances, Bongo became an important element in the strip, reflecting Matt's point of view from a child's perspective and Binky and Sheba's growing anxiety and frustration as his parents. While Bongo's illegitimacy did not set well with some readers, he defended Bongo's origin by poking fun at some classic cartoon characters: "Making Bongo illegitimate is actually very much in the tradition of cartooning. I mean, who is Swee'pea's dad? We all recognize it's Popeye. And what about Huey, Dewey, and Louie? Isn't it Donald [Duck]? Those cartoons don't really say. I'm just more forthright about it."

For hundreds of thousands of readers nationwide, the primary reason for picking up alternative news weeklies like *Los Angeles Reader* and *Chicago Reader* and their empire of free satellite weekly arts journals was to read the continuing installments of Matt's hilarious and slyly philosophical cartoon. "The more mean things I did to him [Binky]," he explained, "the more popular he became."

During this period, Matt found the ideal partner, personally and professionally. She was a vivacious, wavy red-haired beauty responsible for taking his career to the next step and beyond. Her name was Deborah Caplan. After joining the *Reader* in 1980, the year Matt was hired, Deborah worked her way up from selling ads in the advertisement department. Starting in 1982, she was promoted to sales manager of the department, the same year she and Matt began dating. Calling him "the coolest of them all," she developed a deep appreciation for him and quickly saw his potential. As she remembered, "I didn't take many sales calls before I realized that Groening's comic strip was the major drawing card for the newspaper."

A perfect match, Matt and Deborah fell in love. Deborah not only became his girlfriend but also eventually his business partner and manager. Matt credits her with straightening out his chaotic artist lifestyle and turning him into a mini-business empire encompassing books, coffee cups, T-shirts, and other spin-offs of his *Life in Hell* characters ("Half the credit goes to her," he said). Before then, living in "the singles capital of the world" gave Matt plenty of grist for his cartoons, unlike the safer comforts of a happily married man, which he pored into future strips along with many aspects of "hell" intruding into daily life.

In 1984, Matt expanded his cartoon strip, unveiling identical, cantankerous roommates and characters from his childhood, Akbar and Jeff, first appearing in the background of his strip. He was unusually coy for many years in explaining the exact nature of their relationship until he finally admitted, "I say they are either brothers or lovers or possibly both. But they're gay."

The following year, the perfectly matched, fez-topped, and Charlie Brown T-shirt and short-clad pair rose to prominence. This was after hawking the first of many entrepreneurial ventures that seemed surprisingly sensible. One of them was Akbar and Jeff's trendy Tofu Hut in a strip published in around 40 publications that created a surprising reaction. Readers of two papers in Santa Barbara and Hermosa Beach, California, actually called the papers' editors and said, "I saw your ad for Tofu Hut and I've been looking for it, where is it?" As Matt joked with one reporter, "I guess I can't understand someone wanting to try Earth Juice and a Tatershake and a Tofustada, or to chew some Tofooey—nature's taffy."

Occasionally, Matt ran into a little trouble from using his real-life experiences with his ex-girlfriends in drawing his strip. A couple of them once called him and asked, "Is that me?" For the most part, readers responded favorably to his humorous trials and tribulations of love and romance, no matter "how off-base" he said they got. "I like to think my own stuff has some element of insight in it," he explained. "My own problems about love are tragic, and everybody else's is hilarious."

Matt was content in doing his strip only weekly. It allowed him to do other things creatively. Besides freelancing as a music critic to "fill in the gaps left by rock critics," he successfully filled another void: writing a biography of his favorite rock musician Frank Zappa, *Mother! Is the Story of Frank Zappa*, published in November 1984, by Proteus Publishing. Gaining greater notoriety, Matt started holding public showings of his work at small galleries in Los Angeles and elsewhere. That June, he held his first major exhibit east of the Rockies at the Olshonsky Gallery, one of the nation's most prestigious galleries, in Washington, D.C. Other successful showings followed.

By July 1984, Matt's *Life in Hell* strip had increased its readership. It now appeared weekly in the *Washington City Paper* and 11 dailies, from Seattle to Baltimore. A critic for the *Washington Post* praised the 30-year-old cartoonist's comical bent on weighty subjects, from the working man to children's science experiments, as "forthright and uncomfortably funny." Matt said he owed his modicum of success to the "degeneration" of the industry that had begun a few years earlier with the transformation of cartoons on all levels, from daily strips to children's comic books to underground cartoons, in spite of the slow degeneration in drawing quality of many cartoonists. "If you think we draw bad, just wait until 10 years from now," he retorted, "and see the people coming along who are influenced by us."

Whether by design or by fate, Matt's haphazardly drawn and usually frank strip helped fuel a huge underground movement and new wave of alternative comics that gradually enjoyed a groundswell of support from readers across all age groups. While this new style of cartoon did not represent the majority, it would become increasingly popular and respected. This was especially the case as public tastes and perceptions of the art form changed with the times. Matt noted, ". . . It's just like the television line from 'Ernie Kovacs' to 'Laugh-In' to 'Saturday Night Live' changed things. A sense of humor really builds up in a community of people before certain editors, producers, and people in the media acknowledge it by bringing in two or three new faces and then it suddenly goes wild."

Consequently, Matt joined an emerging class of cartoonists who successfully made comics more about ideas than art while challenging the belief systems of their readers under the veil of humor.

GROWING HIS CARTOON EMPIRE

With *Life in Hell* developing a cult following, Matt's dynamic and driven partner Deborah sought to expand his comic empire. In November, she offered to publish his cartoons as a book, which she financed, called *Love Is Hell*. Matt's idea for the book sprang from an earlier episode in his life that predated Deborah. After breaking up with his then current girlfriend, he miserably drew three words, "Love is Hell." Afterward, he said to himself, "There, I never have to go through that again."

Those three scribbled words became the basis of his latest book. Published that December, the oversized paperback anthology—his first book sharing, as he explained, his "most painful and intimate feelings" by his weirdly drawn rabbit Binky—featured love and relationship-themed panels from his earlier strips divided into 13 chapters. The book became a huge underground success. It sold 22,000 copies in its first two printings.

The book's remarkable sales gave Matt hope that his strip was catching fire with audiences. As a follow-up, he wrote an equally successful sequel that Deborah also published, a mini-jumbo edition, *Work Is Hell*. The waffle-iron-sized paperback, which he wrote to help him with the mental preparation of quitting his job at the *Reader*, tackled the outright dissatisfaction most people feel about their jobs: "Should I go into business for myself? Is this what I'll be doing for most of my life? And if it is, how can I kill eight hours a day and still keep my job?"

TAKING CONTROL OF HIS ENTERPRISE

Despite the success of his syndicated strip and back-to-back books, Matt and Deborah were barely scraping by. In 1985, each was unhappy in their professional careers. Exhibiting the same foresight that made his two previous books hugely successful, Deborah came up with a plan to take them in a new direction. Quitting their *Los Angeles Reader* jobs, they launched two separate enterprises that led them out of their financial abyss. The first was ACME Features Syndicate, which bypassed major newspaper syndicates by distributing Matt's strip (and later those of his friends and fellow cartoonists Lynda Barry and John Callahan) directly to alternative newspapers throughout the country.

Next they cofounded Life in Hell Cartoon Company, an umbrella company, whose goal, according to Deborah, was to "keep the machine of Matt going" by producing and selling official *Life in Hell* products, including posters, T-shirts, coffee mugs, and greeting cards. Pursuing products and mail-order merchandise of his characters was Deborah's vision. "She did all the legwork to make that happen," remembered former *Los Angeles Reader* freelance photographer Ann Summa, "and she began the merchandising of 'Life in Hell' on T-shirts and cups. She was an incredible businesswoman."

The first weekend in August 1985, Matt was among dozens of notable artists, comic-book creators, and celebrities from the worlds of science-fiction/fantasy, including Marvel Comics editor and writer Jim Shooter and TV's *Lost in Space* star Billy Mumy, invited to attend the widely popular Comic-Con convention at the San Diego Convention and Performing Arts Center. Promoting his appearance, the now-bearded 31-year-old-cartoonist continued to emphasize the importance of cartooning, especially in his case. "Drawing a comic strip seemed a less painful way of conveying my feelings," he stated.

In expanding its readership, the continuing appeal of Matt's suggestive and existential weekly *Life in Hell* strip was its chilly realities of middle-class American life and wildly popular themes—work, love, sex, and death. Sometimes Binky's romantic entanglements, however, greatly offended his readers. Many objected to "the suggestive bedroom scenes" and "off-color language." Defending his work, Matt stated, "People in Los Angeles, as well as San Diegans, are too jaded to be offended. But in a city like, say, Tucson, people have been outraged by some of my stories."

Matt did not draw the strip to shock people, but he wanted to subvert their thinking. In his own words, he wanted to "engage them" and draw them in with humor and then "pull the rug out" from under them. Despite his strip gaining greater traction nationally, he ardently believed the success of underground artists as a whole remained greatly limited and unaccepted because most built their art around unpopular themes of protest. "They're anti-parent, anti-cop and pro-drugs," he said. "I just didn't want to repeat all of that with my strip."

With his relationship with Deborah going "extremely well," Matt stressed that his *Life in Hell* strip was no longer as autobiographical as it first started out. As he joked to reporters, "I'm no longer Binky, just a friend of his."

Matt was about to enjoy the kind of success and recognition that had long eluded him. Beginning in 1986, everything necessary to catapult him to the next level was within his grasp after all the pieces fell into place.

One of the first was a carryover from the previous year. The full-bearded, quirky underground cartoonist landed his first major book deal. With his *Life in Hell* strip now appearing in dozens of hip, urban tabloids and alternative newspapers, the success of his two spin-off anthologies published by Deborah caught the attention of New York's Pantheon Books. Helping pave the way was Pulitzer Prize-winning comic artist extraordinaire Art Spiegelman, who introduced Matt to Pantheon editor Wendy Wolf. Matt had previously been turned down by Vantage, Random House, Ballantine, and others while trying to find a commercial book publisher for his work, but Wolf took him on.

In April 1986, Pantheon republished Matt's first book, *Love Is Hell*, with a first printing of 20,000 copies. The new edition enjoyed even wider distribution than the first edition, selling more than 50,000 copies nationwide. Later that fall, Pantheon reissued Matt's second book, *Work Is Hell*, which also became a bestseller.

Sales of Matt's books, which were sold even in airport newsstands, underscored the sudden popular acceptance of his work and his strip, as did growing sales of licensed merchandise through his and Deborah's company. Merchandise included numerous spin-offs, like a 1986 calendar, signed lithographs, a miniature rubber Binky doll, and more. The widening appeal of Matt's strip to his growing legion of followers—dubbed "Binkyphiles"—was largely because his work carried, as he stated, "a strong, individual point of view, not standard one-liners."

For the first time, Matt's career began to click on all cylinders and little seemed to be standing in his way. At times, he could not believe he was able to pay his rent from simply "drawing rabbits." For a guy who basically could not draw anything but rabbits, he considered himself fortunate.

Then, on April 23, 1986, Matt suffered a surprise setback. That morning, without warning, the *Los Angeles Reader* dumped his *Life in*

Hell strip after publishing his 300th strip, a move that greatly disappointed him. He had worked for them for seven years. On his way to the airport that day, he picked up the latest edition and saw his strip had been replaced. To this day, he still does not understand why he was let go and remains baffled by their method. As he told writer Richard von Busack, "It's a mystery. I think it has something to do with money, and the fact that I wrote a disgruntled letter to the editor about them firing another writer."

Matt's account of his dismissal only tells part of the story. In February 1985, Vowell, with whom he had worked closely since the publication's origin, accepted an offer to become president and publisher of the *Pasadena Weekly*. Shortly after his departure, David Addison Hawley was installed as the *Reader's* new publisher, replacing Levine and relocating the publication from its offices on Melrose near La Cienega to Laurel Avenue and Victory Boulevard in North Hollywood. According to Conrad Heiney, who filled Matt's old job starting in August 1986, Matt was unable to make a deal with Hawley to continue publishing the strip. As Heiney explained, "I remember people morosely saying, 'Everything has gone to s—t here since we lost the Bunny [Binky].'"

Now a book editor who lives in Yucaipa, California, Vowell, who later bought and owned the *Reader* for almost eight years with his wife Codette Wallace, remembers the same sequence of events. But after Matt got into a dispute with Hawley, Matt took his strip to the more prosperous *LA Weekly* besides freelancing as a music critic for them.

For Matt, the setback proved only temporary. Putting her heart and soul into his work, Deborah turned *Life in Hell* into a lucrative cottage industry. By September 1986, her efforts to expand distribution started to pay off, with 60 publications, mostly alternative newsweeklies and some college papers, carrying his cartoon strip. Daily newspapers, on the one hand, presented a huge stumbling block. Many, except for the *San Francisco Chronicle* and the *Oregonian*, considered the strip "too racy" to publish. "At one point the *Oregonian* was only going to carry it," Matt related, "if I changed the name to 'Life in Heck,'" but they changed their minds. Their decision of the dailies smacked with hypocrisy since many—including the *San Francisco Chronicle* and East Coast papers like the *Hartford Courant* and the *Washington Post*—had been running Bill Griffith's syndicated *Zippy* cartoon strip since 1985. *Zippy* satirized the excesses of consumerism. Many readers found the unpredictable behavior of its polka-dotted, puffy-white-shoed, pinheaded clown star "reprehensible." Matt added, "If *Zippy* can get into daily newspapers, then we know values are crumbling and civilization will be ready for *Life in Hell* someday."

Throughout this period, producers took notice of the skyrocketing success of Matt's *Life in Hell* strip. Matt and Deborah received several inquiries from movers-and-shakers in the television industry about adapting the strip into a weekly cartoon series. But Matt proved to be a tough bargainer. He was not about to relinquish the rights to his characters unless any series met certain standards—his. In meeting with television executives, he talked about how "bad" TV cartoons were and how he wanted to do something with the same standards as the 1960s cult favorites, Rocky and Bullwinkle—"great writing, great voices, great music." Executives instantly turned cold and distant, calling that show "a failure" because it only appealed to "smart kids." Instead they said, "We're trying to appeal to the 3- to 5-year-old market."

Shocked and surprised, Matt, who was entirely new to the business, asked, "So why did you call me in? I draw a comic strip called *Life Is Hell*."

They soon showed him the door.

Feeling that viewers were thirsting for such a smart, animated show, Matt held firm. It was a decision he would never regret and that would later play out in his favor, forever altering the landscape of television and pushing his career to staggering levels of fame and fortune.

The Doodler God Makes Good

O ne day, in late 1985, Matt received a phone call from someone he least expected: Hollywood film and television producer James L. Brooks, famous for his work on *The Mary Tyler Moore Show, Taxi,* and *Terms of Endearment.* Brooks contacted him about the prospects of working in animation on an "undefined future project."

Matt was surprised Brooks knew who he was. It turned out he was a huge fan of his *Life in Hell* strip. An anonymous admirer of Matt's work had unknowingly planted the seeds that would produce the opportunity Matt had long desired. Movie producer Polly Platt, then working for Brooks's company, bought original art to one of his strips and gave it to Brooks as a gift. The 1982 strip, titled "The Los Angeles Way of Death," covered the 12 best ways to die in Los Angeles. Platt's friendly gesture provided a few hearty laughs for Brooks, who never forgot the strip or its creator. "I had this great *Life in Hell* cartoon on my wall," Brooks remembered, "so I thought of Matt."

Brooks set up a date to meet with Matt at his office, which was then on the Paramount Studios lot where he produced both *Taxi* and *Cheers.* Matt lived right next door, still in his same roach-infested, one-bedroom apartment. He was struggling financially at the time. He was again carless, as his had broken down, so he walked from his apartment to the studio. Reaching the front gate, the guard asked incredulously, "Where is your car?"

"I don't have one," Matt shrugged.

Informing him of his appointment with Brooks, the guard ushered him inside.

Unlike other television executives, Brooks did not show Matt the door. In their first meeting, he explained he was developing a new comedy/variety show, starring British comedienne Tracey Ullman, through his company, Gracie Films. The show would be for Rupert Murdoch's new start-up or "fourth network," FOX Broadcasting Company (simply known as FOX), set to launch in October 1986. He wanted to feature a series of animated skits on Ullman's program and asked Matt to come up with some ideas.

Fast forward to 1986: Matt met Brooks, then holed up in a tiny bungalow of his Gracie Films offices at 20th Century Fox Studios where Ullman's show was to be taped. This time they were also meeting with FOX executives. Matt was given only two minutes in which to pitch his ideas to them and audition for the job.

Sitting outside Brooks's office, Matt intended to pitch his *Life in Hell* rabbit characters, but he stopped short. He thought, "I'm not going to give this up. I can't give this up. This is my bread and butter."

Despite the fact he was poor, carless, and lived in a hellhole of an apartment, he had put eight long years into the strip and was not bound to let it go so easily. Furthermore, if his first effort in animation failed, he did not want to subject his own characters to such failure, the ramifications of which could be quite damaging to the franchise. So he thought, "I'd better make up some new ones."

Matt grabbed his trusty cartoonist pen and paper and started drawing "really fast." In 15 minutes flat, he drew what he termed as a crude, ugly, badly dressed family. They were his decidedly perverse take on popular family sitcoms of his youth, with bulging eyes and severe overbites. He named them after his own family—a father, Homer; a mother, Marge, after his mom Margaret; two younger sisters, Lisa and Maggie; and a son he initially wanted to name Matt. Since, as he put it, that would have "given the game away . . . I didn't want you to think that it was autobiographical," he called him Bart instead, an anagram for "brat." Bart was based on his older brother, Mark ("There, I've said it!"). He called them "The Simpsons."

Matt has admitted drawing his characterizations of Homer and Marge, respectively, from various childhood influences, including *The Flintstones*. "Those large 'rocks' that Marge has around her neck are definitely inspired by Wilma Flintstone's necklace," he explained. "Homer's beard line was definitely influenced by Fred Flintstone, although very early on in *The Simpsons*, some people didn't understand that it was a beard line. I got this letter from an outraged woman who said, 'What is that horrible man with the gigantic lips?'"

Matt decided early on that Lisa would be the sensitive one in the family, an angst-ridden second-grader who wanted nothing more than, as he described, "peace on earth, good will toward men, and well, okay, maybe a pony." Otherwise the similarities end there. Unlike their cartoon counterparts, Matt's real-life family was more laid-back, less feisty. His father was not fat and bald; his mother never had three feet of blue hair, though she once sported a hairdo that looked immense from his perspective as a kid. As he revealed, "If I had it to do over again, I probably wouldn't name them after my family. I imagine the guy that Fred Flintstone was named after feels pretty bad."

Although what germinated that day on paper eventually became a signature franchise synonymous with his name around the world, Matt actually originated The Simpsons characters in high school. He featured them in a bleak, unpublished *Catcher in the Rye*-type novel he wrote, titled *The Mean Little Kids*. The story centered on a teenage Bart Simpson with buckteeth and a bad complexion, and a father, Homer, named after a character in American novelist Nathanael West's *The Day of the Locust*. As he later joked, ". . . there is an actual literary reference in there somewhere."

Matt nervously finished the drawings just before Brooks called him in. After exchanging pleasantries, he told Brooks straight up, "You can't have my bunnies."

Instead, Matt pitched his idea of an off-kilter, suburban American cartoon family more in step with the way families really were in his view. Brooks immediately loved the concept. But, before hiring him, he had to convince network executives. Lobbying hard on his behalf, Brooks won out. He brought Matt on board to develop his spur-of-the-moment renderings into full-fledged animated segments for Ullman's show.

Matt shared his good news with those closest to him, including his longtime friend cartoonist Lynda Barry. With Barry, he had tried fulfilling another long-held dream of becoming a screenwriter that year by putting ideas down for a script with her for a romantic comedy. Like "only we could," Barry told a reporter laughingly at the time.

The same year, on October 29, Matt and Deborah were married in front of family and friends. Foregoing the usual plastic bride and groom figurines, they appropriately topped their tiered wedding cake with clay replica figurines of *Life in Hell*'s Binky and his girlfriend, Sheba, instead.

Meanwhile, on November 19, additional details were leaked to the press about FOX's slate of new original programming. That included news of Brooks's yet-untitled half-hour series—eventually announced as *The Tracey Ullman Show*—starring the bouncy British comedienne and bringing her character-driven comedy act to American television. FOX was banking on Ullman bringing her "Midas touch" in television, film, and records to its fledgling network. While ostensibly the star attraction, she was to be joined by a small ensemble cast: Emmy Award-winning actress Julie Kavner (of TVs *Rhoda* fame as Rhoda's sister), Dan Castellaneta, Jeffrey Essman, and Bob Nelson. The show would present an unsettling collection of unconventional sketches, variety-show acts, song parodies, and guest entertainers, combining character comedy and music. Castellaneta and Kavner were signed on to perform dual roles—in live-action sketches and as the voices of dad Homer and mother Marge in Matt's dysfunctional cartoon vignettes.

On March 18, 1987, Matt and Brooks auditioned actors for Bart and Lisa. Nancy Cartwright, the only *Simpsons* cast member trained in voice acting, and Yeardley Smith tried out for the role of Bart. Originally Cartwright intended to read for the middle child, Lisa, but was drawn more to the part of the devious, underachieving, school-hating, irreverent son. So Matt let her try out for the part of Bart. Smith, who always read and sounded "too much like a girl," landed the part of Lisa, and Matt hired Cartwright on the spot as Bart.

Recording the mini-cartoon episodes was rather primitive in the beginning. The cast recorded their dialogue on a portable tape deck in a makeshift studio above the bleachers in the sound stage on the 20th Century Fox lot where *The Tracey Ullman Show* was filmed.

Matt's greatest challenge from the start was adapting his loosely structured cartoon style into a completely linear story and for animators to make a series of 15- to 20-second spots each following an individual story. He was not alone in this effort. Out of the artists he also auditioned, Brooks hired another cartoonist, M. K. Brown, to showcase her mostly verbal style featuring highly rendered characters in a series of limited animation shorts alternating every other week with Matt's, called *Dr. N!Godatu*.

Matt storyboarded, scripted, and produced each segment of his in collaboration with Klasky Csupo, a small, independent, Hollywood animation studio Brooks hired. Klasky Csupo also animated Brown's segments. Director and studio cofounder Gabor Csupo produced animation for about a quarter of what it typically cost—proving it was possible to produce adult-themed animation without sacrificing quality. Each series was animated in its creator's style by Csupo's staff of three talented animators: David Silverman, Wes Archer (both of whom later directed episodes of the weekly *The Simpsons* series), and Bill Kopp.

INTRODUCING AMERICA'S NEWEST CARTOON FAMILY

Following its Sunday, April 5, 1987, premiere, over time *The Tracey Ullman Show* became a solid hit for FOX, giving the network some much-needed credibility. The multitalented firecracker Ullman won the affection of audiences young and old with her remarkable collection of characters and vignettes. One critic noted that they were like "a little Lucy . . . some Jackie Gleason, some Carol Burnett, Milton Berle, and a bit of Ernie Kovacs."

Inspired by members of his family, Matt created crude, spur-of-the-moment drawings of a dysfunctional lower middle-class family, to become known as The Simpsons, for a series of animated bits on James L. Brook's *The Tracey Ullman Show* for the newly launched FOX network.

Matt's animated bits of his irreverent offspring actually fared poorly with test audiences. It was not until the segments were later played in sequence on the Ullman's series that, as he admitted, "a strangely attractive narrative" began to emerge. On April 19, 1987, two weeks later, his cartoon interstitials made their national television premiere. Drawn in the same primitive style of his surrealistic comic strip, *Life in Hell*, *The Simpsons* segments, each featuring a punch line and payoff at the end, played at various points in the program during the show's first two seasons. They also appeared in the show's opening theme, giving Ullman a hearty "Hi." During the first season, Homer and Marge were simply called Dad and Mom, and then as Mr. Simpson and Mrs. Simpson in the second season. Not until the third season of Ullman's program were they called by their rightful first names. The last people to know about his creations were Matt's family. As he confessed, "I didn't tell my family, just told them to tune in [the first] Sunday night. My parents pretended to be proud."

In the premiere episode, "Good Night," Marge blithely sang "Rock-a-Bye Baby" to her little daughter Maggie, who was sucking on her pacifier in bed. Maggie interprets the lyrics literally and imagines herself cradled in a treetop that crashes to the ground. Liz George voiced baby Maggie's gurgled "g'night" in the opening episode. In the shorts and earlier series episodes, Castellaneta, as Homer, modeled his voice after that of actor Walter Matthau. Later, during the second and third seasons of the half-hour series *The Simpsons*, he modified Homer's voice to a more robust version, allowing him a fuller range of expression and emotions.

In the beginning, animators more or less traced Matt's oversized original storyboards to draw the characters. After they developed into their own weekly series, the designs and layouts of his animated family radically changed with their trademark "Simpsons drawing style" evolving. "I thought, 'You know, it's kind of Thurberesque,'" Matt said of those early Ullman shorts. "But after I saw the first episodes, I realized we'd have to work harder to define exactly what we wanted. Also, it was very low-budget. After two seasons, we got more support."

Matt and his fellow writers and animators started off small with seven cartoon shorts in Ullman's first season. The miniscule format barely afforded them enough time to develop a joke or sight gag, much less fully establish the characters. At first, audiences and critics found his grotesque, bucktoothed family "unfunny and intrusive." As writer Gregory Solman of *Millimeter* magazine wrote: "Generally people liked *The Tracey Ullman Show* or *The Simpsons*, not both."

Dubbed by one critic as a "skitcom" for its high number of comedy skits, Ullman's variety show overcame a shaky start, with the 27-year-old comedienne and her writers frequently tweaking the show to best use her abundant talent. As her characterizations grew sharper and funnier, so did Matt's skew on the all-American family and suburban anxieties in his weekly Simpsons segments, which one critic crowed added "a hipper, absurdist edge" to the program. The more they aired, the more people laughed and the more they liked them. For Matt, the transition from cartooning to animation was natural and fulfilling, yet part of another longtime vow: that he would work every medium available to him. "I've yet to write a good novel or an opera," he stated then. "So far I've concentrated on the low-end greeting cards, comic strips, merchandise and TV—the lowest end."

Admitting how the "frivolity of drawings rabbits" had gotten to him, Matt still wanted to write something that would be taken more seriously. That year, he completed writing a "light" novel based on his early struggles in Los Angeles, called *Hipness and Stupidity*. He began writing the book to overcome, as he described, "the stigma of being a cartoonist," but it was never published. When asked by a reporter if the "world was ready for a novel from the author of *Life in Hell*," the normally laid-back cartoonist, fiddling with his cartooning pen, smirked and said, "Someday they'll realize that I'm not a cartoonist. I'm a doodle god."

During that year, thanks to Deborah's remarkable business savvy and marketing sense and the added national exposure of his work on Ullman's show, Matt's bulgy-eyed Binky and his crazy crew soared to new heights. His *Life in Hell* strip not only was published in 65 newspapers by that November, but also spurred a tremendous boom of licensed merchandise of his oddball characters surfacing everywhere. "I thought the characters were too obnoxious for anybody to wear," Matt admitted then. "I was wrong. Now, all I want is a rubber Binky to play with, and I'll be happy man."

Mining the successful formula of his *Life in Hell* strip, that April, Matt penned his third compendium for Pantheon, *School Is Hell*. He ransacked high school dumpsters for notebooks and papers that students trashed at the end of the school year for material. His primary motivation in doing a book about his hellish school days was to "make times of misery pay off." The final product was full of witty observations and savvy advice on such topics as "Trouble: Getting In and

Weaseling Your Way Out" and "How to Drive a Deserving Teacher Crazy." One strip devoted to kindergarten even explains how to "gun out" a cookie: "Grab a cookie. Bite the cookie into the shape of a gun. Fire when ready."

In late May, at that year's American Booksellers Association (ABA) convention at the vast Washington Convention Center in Washington, D.C., Matt's publisher, Pantheon, took a guerilla marketing approach to launching his latest book. They distributed buttons to passersby on the convention room floor that pictured a perspiring Binky weighted down by bags of free books and other booty, groaning, "ABA Is Hell."

On October 4, *School Is Hell* skyrocketed to third in *The Seattle Times* weekly list of bestsellers in the Pacific Northwest—with his previously reissued *Love Is Hell* ranking sixth—in the category of Food/Advice/Humor paperbacks. Matt made the rounds promoting and signing the book, including an appearance in early November at the Miami Book Fair International. Then, just in time for the Christmas rush, Random House, the parent company of Pantheon, published his first widely available 12-month wall calendar, the *Life in Hell 1988 Fun Calendar*, providing more hilarious fun culled from his strip.

While ideas for future titles ran deep, the good-natured, neatly bewhiskered, 33-year-old cartoon wonder admitted in 1987 that even he had his limits. "I don't think I'll ever do a book called, 'Golf Is Hell,'" he said.

Awash in success, the roach-infested apartment Matt once called home and where he had stashed his pencils to draw his strip had been left behind. Earlier that year, he and Deborah had begun making Venice their new home ("It's the only air in L.A. that is remotely breathable," he stated). The couple now lived in a small, comfy one-bedroom cottage fronting the canals of this funky Los Angeles beach town populated by two kinds of residents—"those who ride bicycles and those who stagger," Matt mused. Matt gave credit where credit was due for the move. Pointing to his wife, he told an interviewer, "She's the one who got me out of my miserable Hollywood apartment."

From their beachfront home, Matt either bicycled or drove in his Subaru the one mile to his beachside studio, a garage he had converted into a grown-up, decorated version of "a little boy's clubhouse" that he called his "Bat Cave." There he worked on his strip while seated at a drafting table next to a disheveled desk with a battered blue notebook labeled "HELL" lying atop it. Along with a beat-up sofa, the cluttered work space, with vintage books, comic books, and records piled high around him and posters plastered on its walls, offered him all the practical tools to be creative.

Matt's studio was only a short drive from ACME Features Syndicate and Life in Hell Cartoon Co. headquarters on trendy Main Street in downtown Santa Monica. There, with displays of Matt's google-eyed alter-ego Binky inside, Deborah oversaw its operation and their three employees in licensing and distributing *Life in Hell*. By December 1988, it was appearing in 94 publications, alternative weeklies, and metropolitan dailies. She also oversaw distribution of merchandise to gift and college markets. Explaining their business style, Matt said, "We feed each other. I feed them material, and they get everything out. It's all distribution."

Despite his sudden success, Matt was not worried about his well of "hellish" elements in his daily life suddenly drying up to keep his quirky characters or comic strip going. "To some extent," the artist said, "your attitude changes when you're able to pay the rent instead of not being able to pay the rent."

Matt was more willing to seek out "sticky situations" in future installments. As Deborah joked with an interviewer, "He likes to irritate people. He likes to cause controversy. He likes to cause drama, in the true sense of the staunch liberal he is."

EARNING THE RESPECT OF HIS PEERS

On September 20, 1987, two days before its second-season premiere, FOX's *The Tracey Ullman Show* figured prominently at the Academy of Television Arts & Sciences annual prime-time Emmy Awards held at the Pasadena Civic Auditorium. Industry peers demonstrated their obvious affection for the multifaceted comedienne and her series, nominating the show for five awards for its first season. Matt earned his first Emmy nomination for "Outstanding Writing in a Variety or Music Program," along with the series' fellow writers, for their writing of three episodes.

For the naturally brown-haired and bespectacled cartoonist, who was more accustomed to dressing like a self-described "poverty-stricken slob" in characteristically untucked T-shirts, baggy pants, and Hush Puppies, the event marked one of the rare times he wore a suit and tie. In a brief moment of naïveté, when the studio informed him they would send a limo for him, he asked, "Do I pick it up at the studio?"

"You don't understand," the voice on the other end said, "We send the limo to *you.*"

By 1988, Matt became something of an industry rarity—an underground cartoonist who had successfully made the leap to commercial cartoonist. By the second season of *The Tracey Ullman Show*, *The Simpsons* became the series' most popular segment, a fact that surprised even its creator. "Nobody thought *The Simpsons* was going to be a big hit," Matt confided. "It sneaked up on everybody." Furthermore, in distinguishing itself as a cornerstone of the program's overall success, Matt was no longer known to a small, enthusiastic constituency as "the guy who does *Life in Hell*," but on a much larger scale as "the guy who created *The Simpsons.*"

That season, *The Simpsons* went from being featured in 7 animated segments to 22 in all. As the cartoon shorts developed, Matt introduced other supporting characters that later became essential parts of FOX's weekly series, including Grampa, Krusty the Clown, and Itchy and Scratchy.

The success of his cartoon creations turned his and Deborah's lives upside down. "It bumped Matt and Deborah up to the stratosphere," said former *Los Angeles Reader* employee Jeff Spurrier, who met Matt at the paper in 1979, "and out of our grimy 'L.A. Reader' existence."

By the spring of 1988, Matt and Deborah celebrated more good news when she announced she was pregnant with their first child. Matt's parents were particularly excited over the news of their middle son's pending fatherhood, especially since now, as they told him, the "tables will be turned."

Matt with wife Deborah, eight-month old son, Homer, and their pet duck, Brownie, outside their one-bedroom cottage on the canals of Venice Beach in 1989. © *Time & Life Pictures*. *Photo by Mark Sennet/Onyx*.

In the late fall, on November 5, 1988, Matt welcomed yet another new addition to his growing cartoon empire, his fourth hot-off-the-presses *Life in Hell* book, *Childhood Is Hell*, by signing and hawking copies at the Annex of The Catbird Seat Bookstore on Taylor Street in downtown Portland. Based partly on his fifth-grade diary and written to help prepare him for the birth of his first son, this latest collection—preceded by a gift set that hit bookstores in late October 1988, *Box Full of Hell*—contained 48 of the wittiest and weirdest cartoons from his strip presented in 25 chapters. Delighted to be published in the same company as Pantheon's leading literary figures, including famous French philosopher Jean-Paul Sartre and Pulitzer Prize-winning American author Studs Terkel, Matt called himself "the goofball on the list."

Childhood Is Hell became Matt's fourth bestseller. By the end of December, his four books totaled one million copies in print, combined, and became popular sellers in England, France, and Germany as well. Reviews of his literary collections were mostly favorable. *Los Angeles Times Book Review* critic Charles Solomon wrote that "while Groening's artwork is not great in the traditional sense, it serves as a vehicle for good writing and sharp wit" and added that he "is one of the funniest and most original cartoonists working in the comics today." Of Matt's cartooned obsessions, Richard Harrington of the *Washington Post* offered: "It's funny and fatalistic, rude and revealing, touching raw nerves, funny bones and heartstrings all at the same time."

During national book tours, Matt signed books and chatted up close and personal with fans of his work, mostly college students and young adults disillusioned with the world who had become huge cult followers of his strip. Often, he personalized each book with a drawing of Binky next to his signature.

With his cartoon groanings, now published in 103 publications by mid-summer, becoming a national phenomenon, Matt and Deborah's Life in Hell Cartoon Company began yielding them an income of more than six-figures annually. It was a far cry from the meager earnings he made toiling as an editor and columnist for the *Los Angeles Reader*. As he told an interviewer, "Everyone I know goes, 'Well, if I had a Deborah, I could be a success, too.' And they're right."

Humbled by his success, the happily and hopelessly warped cartoonist took it in stride. "I'm a writer who just happens to draw," he stated. Gesturing to his drawing board while showing a reporter his crudely drawn strip, he added, with a bemused smile on his face, "I mean, look, you could do this."

EVOLVING INTO SOMETHING SPECIAL

On *The Tracey Ullman Show* that season, it became increasingly obvious to producer James L. Brooks that Matt's rather strange cartoon family had evolved into something much more valuable. During tapings of her program, the live studio audiences reportedly grew hostile waiting for Ullman—who spent two-and-a-half hours in makeup to transform herself into the different characters she played—to perform what amounted to around 20 minutes of entertainment in two or three comedy playlets per half-hour. Performing in each skit meant makeup and costume changes each time, resulting in tremendous lag time in between. Brooks decided to stitch together Matt's little cartoon pieces of *The Simpsons* and show them to keep the audience entertained. As he once said, that "invariably got the best laughs of the night, even though Tracey was brilliant and we did okay."

By the third season of Ullman's program in November 1988, instead of being shown as separate segments, Matt bizarre characters were featured in entire one-and-a-half minute shorts—19 in all—between the show's live-action sketches each week. The new format more successfully drew out the distinctive characteristics and humor of his breezily dysfunctional characters and produced an even greater response from audiences.

In interviews that July promoting the series' third season launch, Matt began referring to his unusual, homely-looking characters as "the Simpson family." As he mischievously confided in an interview that November while slurping on tapioca pudding from a parfait glass at Du-Par's Restaurant and Bakery near Los Angeles's historic Farmers Market, "My sister did say she saw a wee bit of Bart in me." Later in the season, the characters were to star in their own five-minute "cartoonlette" and, if successful, be expanded to a half-hour special and maybe a weekly series.

Every time he drove from his ACME Features Syndicate office to 20th Century Fox Studios, Matt still got a thrill entering the studio gates. Prior to his success on Ullman's show, the closest he got to seeing the inside of a studio was driving by the front gates on his way to some crummy job and wondering, "What's the secret?"

Offers to commercialize Matt's odd cartoon family soon began to pour in. In January 1989, they were featured in two commercials produced by New York's Lintas agency, whose clients include many Fortune 500 companies—one for Butterfinger candy bars (with discussions begun back in November) and another for Planters Life Savers candy. While acknowledging his surprise over commercial interest in his characters, he was pleased the agency never put any restrictions on his creative input. Likewise he was delighted by the success of both franchises, *The Simpsons* and *Life in Hell*, seen in 105 papers by year's end. "I think they could coexist in the same universe," he told the *New York Times* that year, "but *Life in Hell* is me in a bad mood and *The Simpsons* is me in a nostalgic mood."

That spring, his final season on Ullman's show, Matt and his fellow writers were recognized with another Emmy nomination but lost for the third time. Then, in April, he and Deborah became parents for the first time when she gave birth to a baby boy. Matt named him Homer, after his farther, "in part trying to prove to my dad that I had the best intentions. I wasn't trying to get back at him for some perceived slight."

By the time Homer was eight months old, the family had moved into a much larger home—a white-picket fenced, two-bedroom cottage with double French doors off the back deck—on the canal in Los Angeles's coastal suburb of Venice, with their pet duck, Brownie. It was a move the then 35-year-old, socially savvy cartoonist admitted he was reluctant to make. He was too concerned that the mortgage on the place was "too bourgeois," until his much more practical wife pointed out he could "canoe from his front door."

That season, Matt huddled with Brooks, producer-writer Sam Simon, a brilliant sitcom writer who developed many previous projects with Brooks, and a virtual army of animators, to develop a half-hour pilot based on *The Simpsons* for a weekly series produced by Brooks's company. The concept they created was that of a blue-collar sitcom set in a small, mythical and surreal Midwestern town, Springfield, a burg much like Matt's native Portland, with a scenic gorge, a nuclear power plant, toxic waste dump, and a polluted river nearby. The town's fictitious name was inspired by Matt's memories of Robert Young's idyllic 1950s sitcom, *Father Knows Best*, which he had watched as a kid and which had its own Springfield address, and growing up next to Springfield, Oregon, not far from his childhood home.

Each story would follow the comical exploits of Matt's revolting-looking lower-middle-class suburban family, largely intact from Ullman's show:

- the crude, overweight, incompetent, and ignorant family patriarch and ineffectual husband and father, Homer, a safety inspector at the local nuclear power plant and better known as "Bonehead" to his bosses
- the voice of reason, his craggy-voiced wife, Marge, who settles the many family squabbles and whose most striking feature is her towering blue beehive hair
- their simply horrid, ham-fisted, loudmouthed 10-year-old son, Bart, who works hard at nonconformity
- their gratingly precocious second-grade daughter—and a whiz on the saxophone—Lisa
- and their infant daughter, Maggie, who never utters a sound other than making loud sucking noises with her pacifier

Voicing the characters were Ullman show holdovers Dan Castellaneta, Julie Kavner, Nancy Cartwright, and Yeardley Smith as Homer, Marge, Bart, and Lisa, respectively.

Matt pitched *The Simpsons* in a meeting with Barry Diller, then chairman of FOX Network. At first, Diller was not wild about the idea. Producing hand-drawn animation was labor-intensive and expensive, and Diller had trepidations about committing that kind of resources to the series. In the course of their meeting, he curiously asked Matt, "So where is this Springfield located?"

Matt readily responded, "Well, I think it's vaguely some mythical town in the Midwest."

Diller, nodding, agreed. "Yeah, it could be."

It was then that Matt realized Springfield was really, in his words, "a state of mind," and could be almost anywhere, even right there in the San Fernando Valley, and had an everyman appeal about it.

Selling FOX on doing a weekly series was touch and go. As Brooks explained, "We fought for it. FOX took a big chance . . . we asked for a series order, and they wanted specials, and we held out. And they were almost bankrupt then. That was in the early days of the network. We had to wait six months. And they had to take this gamble." In his negotiations with the network, Brooks swayed FOX to sign off on a provision in the contract preventing them from interfering with the show's content, something generally unheard of.

In an interview in April 1990, Diller related that doing the series on the basis of the success of the 48 mini-episodes that aired on Ullman's show seemed like "a huge risk." He tried hard to say, "Oh, let's just do four specials. What do we need to rush so fast for?"

Finally, Diller commissioned a pilot that Brooks's company produced in tandem with Klasky Csupo, FOX's first choice after they outbid several other animation studios, including Film Roman, to once again handle the animation. After seeing a rough cut of the show, he experienced something uncommon in his reaction. "It's not often I've had this experience of watching something great and praying that the next minute doesn't dash it," Diller admitted. "And not only having that not happen, but saying at the end: 'This is the real thing! This is the one that can crack the slab for us!'"

After the advance screening, Diller committed to a full season, ordering 13 half-hour episodes. *The Simpsons* was set to become the first network cartoon series to air in prime-time since Hanna-Barbera's *The Flintstones* in 1960. The latter's cocreator, legendary animator and studio president Joseph Barbera, viewed additional programs in development by various other studios, like *The Simpsons*, as simply "an effort at counter-programming." History would record otherwise. *The Simpsons* would break out to become one of the most successful shows in prime-time television history, with Matt riding on the coattails of its success.

5

Hitting a Homer...D'oh!

For Matt, ten years of hunching over his drawing table in his makeshift Venice garage studio inking his *Life in Hell* cartoon was paying off and well worth the many sacrifices along the way. Now rating his own office at Brooks's company headquarters at 20th Century Fox Studios, he was not only a well-known and household name, but also an executive producer of his own series to boot. Some days it was hard to believe his quirky rabbit characters from the back pages of alternative news weeklies had vaulted him to his own place on prime-time television. After getting sidetracked many times and doing his cartooning as a hobby, "I didn't expect to do this at all," he conceded. "Some hobby!"

Of the recent turn of events in his life, Matt was much more hopeful. As he told the *Los Angeles Times*: "My understanding is that the TV executives who are in power are young enough to remember cartoons as being funny. They have children of their own now, and they wanted to give them something to watch. Part of the reason I'm doing this is that I'm so unhappy with what has been done—animation for TV is about the lowest form of entertainment in existence. There's been an outcry about violence on TV affecting children adversely, what really affects them adversely is bad animation."

65

From the outset, for Matt, Brooks, Simon, and the animation team of Klasky Csupo, expanding the format of *The Simpsons* from 1 minute to 30 minutes and sustaining audience interest while remaining true to what pushed the characters to the forefront was enormously challenging. During development meetings, Brooks told them, "We have to go for real emotion. We have to know what makes these people tick and we have to feel for them. I want people to forget they're watching a cartoon."

Many credit Brooks's strong organizational and storytelling skills to pulling the program together. To say that, however, would give him more credit than due. The final result was a collaborative effort. Matt injected his jaded sensibilities into the characters' development. Simon largely crafted the show's tone and template. Klasky Csupo colorist Georgie Peluse, on the other hand, cooked up the idea of coloring the characters their now-famous Simpsons yellow. Ultimately the platform they invented allowed for all kinds of comedy, including physical sight gags and witty wordplay, with the finished product becoming, as Brooks described, "a normal American family in all of its beauty . . . and all of its horror" with "real emotion."

How critics and audiences would respond to a bigger dose of Matt's darkly funny and not exactly middle-of-the-road family was a much bigger question. Another was would his subversive humor survive in prime time? During a meeting of television critics in the summer of 1989, to unveil the series, Matt, Brooks, and Simon informed the cadre of critics attending that the characters were vastly different from FOX's "unscrupulous and conniving Bundys" in its cutting-edge sitcom, *Married . . . With Children*. As Simon concurred, "They [the Simpsons] don't hate each other. If they do occasionally strangle each other or hit each other over the head, it's just an impulsive act."

Brooks interjected, "Whether they will go over, whether these drawn figures will go over, we don't know."

Adding to the intrigue, Matt described *The Simpsons* as "lovable in a mutant sort of way . . . who because they're animated can be much wilder than live-action families." Contrasting his series—which he described as "an experiment from the word go"—to pioneering prime-time animation shows he watched as a kid, *The Flintstones* and

The Jetsons, and his true inspiration, *Rocky and His Friends,* he added, "We're not doing the same thing as them, but we're aiming for a similar sophistication."

Later, giving his best explanation of all, he defined the concept this way: "There's a lot of humor that's making fun of the abnormal. But I think with *The Simpsons* what we're doing is making fun of people who are normal trying to act normal. Ultimately, they are abnormal. But they're normal average people desperately trying to stay normal. And unable to accomplish that."

Expanding on his thoughts, Matt added, "Sitcoms are about people who live together and say vicious, witty things to each other, which ends up sounding unlike any real character in life. On *The Simpsons* we want to have some of that, but we found it doesn't work if the characters anticipate their own cruelty. If they know in advance they're going to do something mean or mean-spirited, it's no longer funny. But if they're out of control and a victim of their own impulses—so Homer impulsively strangles Bart—it becomes funny. In general, the characters are emotional powder kegs, and they can explode in a second."

FOX was anxious to put the show on sooner—by late September or early October. But with so much strategy and scheming involved in making the show and getting it ready in time, the network did not think the program would be completed by then. "We didn't want to go on just once and go off the air," Matt explained in October 1989. "We only had one or two shows finished. By having a little extra time, we can make some last-minute fixes." Producing the show under an extremely tight schedule, and by people who had never produced this type of show before (". . . particularly me and everyone else. We're learning as we go along"), made it much more challenging.

Richard Raynis, who worked as executive in charge of animation during the show's first season, remembers one problem derailing the show's progress was "a conflict between the live-action sitcom writers/ producers Jim Brooks and Sam Simon and the animators. The show needed to find the right kind of interface to allow both the writers and animators to what they needed to do." As a result, he developed a new working model for *The Simpsons* for how the show was physically

The entire Simpsons family sings, including a Santa-suited Homer, as Grampa Simpson plays the piano in a scene from the first Simpsons program, the half-hour Christmas special, *Simpsons Roasting on an Open Fire*.

produced and managed that greatly influenced how other prime-time and children's programs were made.

Another who helped smooth over the cultural and creative differences between the writers and animators on the series was animator Brad Bird. Joining Klasky Csupo in 1989, he helped develop *The Simpsons* into half-hour programs and directed his first episode in 1990 ("Krusty Gets Busted") and served as an executive consultant on the show for eight seasons. "He was indispensable. He conveyed a love of animation to the writers who were more interested in dialogue and stories," Matt told *Animation Magazine*. "He was also one of the main proponents of the cinematic style that *The Simpsons* ended up pursuing more and more as the years went by. Brad always honored the jokes we came up with, but in as visual a way as possible. Sometimes the writers and I were more concerned about whether the joke was funny at all, rather than whether it was visual or cinematic."

The Simpsons was delayed by unexpected snafus. When FOX executives received the final cut of the first show—the half-hour Christmas special—from the animation studio in South Korea, where final touches were done, they, along with Matt, Brooks, and Simon, were shocked by an outrageous surprise upon screening the show. Apparently, the director and animators had incorporated unauthorized jokes into the program, including an offensive bit about the Simpsons watching a TV show called *The Happy Little Elves Meet the Curious Bear Cubs*, in which a bear cub violently rips off the head of the elf and then giddily drinks his blood. It was "Not exactly a minor addition," as Matt explained. "When we watched it, we sat in the dark for about two minutes in silence. Then we ran for the door. I thought my career in animation had sunk to the bottom of the seas. Had that gotten on the air, there would be no show today."

Consequently, the director (who also did not think some of the early scripts were funny, "so we got rid of them," Matt said) and animators involved were summarily dismissed. Another month lapsed before FOX received the second episode, forcing some merchandisers to postpone shipping products to retailers. Network executives were so appalled by continued quality issues with the writing and animation that they ordered almost 95 percent of the first season to be scrapped and reanimated. Resulting from such production problems, FOX had to shuffle the order of the episodes and push out the premiere date of the Christmas special to December 17. Problems triggered by these events that held up the show put a noticeable strain on the staff.

PRODUCING ANIMATION IS HARD WORK

For Matt, working full time in the animation business with a staff of 50 animators, "all of whom can draw better than I can . . . [and] are able to take my very naïve style and actually do some really funny situations with it," was a huge adjustment for him in the beginning. The need for his constant attention, down to the minutest detail, took up virtually all of his time every week. Often he was forced to draw his *Life in Hell* cartoon strip after midnight, after coming home from the studio. The entire turn of events represented, in his words, "a complete change" in his working style. "I'm used to working in my garage by myself at my drawing board," he said, "and nobody sees my work until it gets sent out and printed, and nobody changes a thing." The opposite was true in television since, in such a creative assembly line, many talented people "have their input in the show."

Displaying a much more casual attitude of his success, Matt considered his involvement in animation a fluke. "Right now it seems that everyone is in awe of the old Warner Bros. cartoons—Tex Avery and those guys. As much as I love that stuff, I decided not to do that look or style à la [*Who Framed*] *Roger Rabbit*," he explained then. "I'd try to make use of the more limited animation and budget that we had. Rocky and Bullwinkle, *George of the Jungle*, all those Jay Ward cartoons are my idea of the best animation that's ever been on television. That's something I definitely thought about."

Calling the show's limited animation "not the most advanced, but does the job," Matt liked how this economical form did not waste energy and motion. As he confessed to a reporter, "That's my problem with a lot of cartoons—all the excess energy expended. It makes me tense just to watch it." Nonetheless, he was excited about the outcome. Beyond the financial gain, his biggest thrill was seeing his doodles that used to get him in trouble at Ainsworth Elementary School and Lincoln High School actually "move and take on a life of their own."

In screening the early *Simpsons* episodes, Matt was surprised by how some of his characters talked and sounded nothing like he thought they would. For instance, his original concept of Bart Simpson was, as he offered, "a much milder, troubled youth given to existential angst" that instead comes off as "a total wiseguy."

In July 1989, touting the upcoming series—listed as "still unscheduled"—to the press, Brooks noted that Matt's quarrelsome clan would be divided on just about everything, "including who gets the first doughnut." In one interview, when asked if this meant television audiences were ready for an animated version of his neurotic rabbit clan, Matt replied, "I think someday that TV will be ready for my hellish stuff." In jest, he suggested that perhaps in a future season Marge Simpson, for some reason, would take off her beehive wig and "reveal her true identity."

Even before the first episode aired, Matt predicted that *The Simpsons* would exceed anything seen on TV's longest-running prime-time cartoon champ, *The Flintstones*. As a six-year-old boy, the prehistoric sitcom did not "grab him" and after a while was just plain "dumb" to him. As he told *TV Host Weekly*, "We think we're pushing the boundaries of what's expected from cartoon shows." Of his first-ever special, he added, "Even though we do some exaggerated stuff, one of our goals is to make people forget they are watching a cartoon for a moment or two and actually care about the characters."

Before the awaited debut of *The Simpsons*, Matt produced a flurry of equally successful and systematically funny follow-up and modestly-priced *Life in Hell* anthologies. In October of that year, Pantheon published his fifth book, *Akbar and Jeff's Guide to Life*, a compendium of comic adventures of his botched-up fifth-grade Charlie Brown characters with fezzes and "eyes on one side of their face" as famously gay and jaunty entrepreneurs who peddle everything from a "Cryonics Hut" ("Do you sincerely want to live forever at a price you can afford?") to the "Airport Snack Bar" ("Relax and enjoy your meal in comfort at one of our contoured plastic eating stations while watching planes refuel and little trucks drive around"). Conversely, *Greetings from Hell*, his first postcard book featuring 32 ready-to-mail postcards of characters from his Life in Hell strip and final book for Pantheon, was published a month later.

On Sunday, December 17, 1989, *The Simpsons'* television era began with "Simpsons Roasting on an Open Fire," showing on FOX at 8:30 P.M. In this first expanded version featuring his squabbling, animated characters (who some kids thought were "monsters," Matt later admitted, because of their grotesque appearance), the story deals with the kinds of problems and tensions families experience at Christmastime.

The Simpsons are faced with a bleak Christmas after Homer learns he will not be awarded a bonus at work, and Marge has to exhaust the family nest egg she has been saving for an emergency. Unfazed, son Bart retorts, "If television has taught me anything, it has taught me that good things always happen at Christmas. It happened to Charlie Brown, it happened to Tiny Tim, and it happened to the Smurfs." The special also featured a recurring character from the Ullman shorts, the rambling, long-winded storyteller, Grampa Simpson, inspired after Matt's real-life grandfather, Abraham Groening.

Piggybacking *America's Most Wanted* and *Married . . . With Children,* Matt's inaugural Simpsons program—later nominated that season for an Emmy Award—placed FOX third for the evening and beat fourth-place ABC. Around Christmas, Matt marked another important mile-stone: publication of his 500th *Life in Hell* strip, which he and Deborah still self-syndicated to hundreds of newspapers. "Not to toot my own horn, [but] I don't think there's any self-syndicated cartoonist in as many papers as I am," he said of the news.

Despite high enthusiasm from both FOX affiliates and adver-tisers, Brooks deemed future weekly installments of *The Simpsons*— which *Newsweek* called "a mutant *Ozzie and Harriet"*—"an incredible roll of the dice." Although the Christmas special underscored Ameri-can's acceptance of Matt's wicked satire in longer form, maintaining that same momentum every week remained uncertain. They had to wait a month to see whether the show, as they say in the business, "had legs."

On Sunday, January 14, 1990, FOX premiered *The Simpsons* in the same 8.30 P.M. prime-time slot. Competing with the second half of CBS's slot-winning *Murder, She Wrote,* NBC's sitcom *My Two Dads,* and ABC's *Free Spirit,* the overnight ratings were as good as everyone had hoped. The half-hour series spin-off debuted at 48th in the ratings, three slots lower than FOX's *Married . . . With Children,* for the first week.

Critical reaction, meanwhile, was all over the map. The *Los Angeles Times* dismissed *The Simpsons* as "a guerilla attack on mainstream TV," while the *Village Voice* called it "the first cathode ray of real brilliance on the horizon of '90s TV." Critic Peter Farrell of the *Oregonian* wrote that

this latest installment wasn't "quite as funny this time as it was in the harder edged Christmas show."

The first week's ratings gave no indication of whether Matt or FOX had a "hit" on its hands, but the second week painted a clearer picture when *The Simpsons* moved up 20 rating points from 48th to tie for 28th. Within two months of its debut, *The Simpsons* accomplished the unthinkable: it made Nielsen's Top 15, hop-scotching an incredible 9 notches from its previous week to 11th, the highest finish *ever* for a program on FOX, for the week ending March 18. This was an astonishing feat since the fledgling network only reached four-fifths of the country.

The Simpsons' surprising success hinged on many people—a talented team of producers, writers, animators, and voice artists—but equally important as them was the one guy or "glue" that held the production together and who understood the characters better than anyone else, their creator, Matt Groening.

MAKING HIS MARK

From the very beginning, Matt was involved in the day-to-day matters of production, with most work being done in a cluster of office suites at Brooks's company—also known as *Simpsons* headquarters—in a small, two-story building on the corner of the 20th Century Fox Studios lot and next to the studios where the then Emmy Award-winning NBC drama *L.A. Law* was filmed. During production of every episode, his workday was exceedingly long, filled with meetings all over town—at the Klasky Csupo animation studio clear across in Hollywood to the FOX studios soundstage back in the other direction in Culver City, a suburb of Los Angeles. Compared to his solitary work as a cartoonist, his work on the show seemed "like one long party," he said, "except it's like a party where you can't go home."

Matt left his imprint on every aspect of every show's creation. He designed the characters. He supervised the team of animators who did the drawings. He worked with the team of writers who wrote the scripts and revised them to "make them funnier." He oversaw the recording sessions with the voice cast as they recorded their dialogue. He also sat in on sessions when the music and sound effects were added. Less an influential Hollywood producer and more like a curious kid, the coolest part of his job was, as he described, "I always feel like it's a little concert being put on just for me." Throughout it all, his main goal was "to make people laugh," he said. "If we can throw in a different point of view, I think that's fine, too."

Unlike the usual crank-it-out approach in producing a live-action sitcom, producing a typical 30-minute *Simpsons* episode normally took six long months—at a cost of around $500,000 per episode—to finish from scripting to meshing the recorded voices of the characters with the animation, from storyboards and sketches to rough and final animation. Recording the cast's lines of dialogue sometimes took 12 hours per show just to get the right effect.

After getting off to a bumpy start, a cornerstone of the show's first season was its writing, something that held true for subsequent seasons. Its crisp characterizations, wildly funny plotlines, and fresh ideas instantly set it apart from anything previously produced for television, animated or otherwise. After the director that was fired had ditched some of the original first season scripts, Matt and the show's writers discovered they could "tell a lot more jokes" and "more story" than people generally did in animation. "The first 13 episodes were really research and we went from there," he said, adding that the show was "very carefully written, and rewritten, and rewritten" to maintain its level of comedy brilliance.

Admittedly, the hardest part in writing the series, Matt found, was keeping the characters "true to themselves." He noted that while animation had "no rules" where characters could simply walk off the end of a cliff, they avoided doing that. "It has to be real," he explained. "It's a constant correcting process, 'No, we can't do that; we can do that!'"

Coproducer Sam Simon credited the show's authenticity to Matt's obsessive attention to details of his childhood that were sometimes "eerie how in touch with his second-grade life he is." During a later recording session in March 1990, for example, after technicians perfected the sound effects for an episode in which Homer and Bart played a video game, Matt insisted that the engineers retool the effect so it sounded less cartoony and "more like a real video game."

Even then, the show suffered its share of quality-control glitches early on. In the main-title drawings of the first shows, Lisa, for some unexplained reason, was shown carrying a banjo case, and other times a tenor sax, even though the "real-life musicians were playing baritones." The idea of Lisa playing the sax started as a lark. Matt thought it would be funny for an eight-year-old girl to play a baritone sax, even though animators did not know what it looked like so its shape and color changed from show to show. In another example, Smithers, Mr. Burns's faithful assistant, was a black character during the first season; in subsequent episodes he was suddenly "white," a problem Matt attributed to "Animation error . . . It was one of the earliest episodes, the third or fourth, and somebody [an animator] made the wrong color choice off a chart. That's the only reason. We like to say that he was on vacation and came back with a tan."

That February, Matt returned like a conquering hero to his hometown of Portland to spray-paint his signature on a huge cartoon mural of Homer and Bart Simpson, created in his honor for his 36th birthday, at the corner of Southwest Fourth Avenue and Burnside. Even local television station KPDX provided a Bart Simpson birthday cake for the festivities. He took the moment to thank his parents and to clarify with a smile that they are "not as stupid or as ugly as the Simpsons."

Matt's parents mostly approved of the show and characters carrying their namesake. Only once did his real-life father, Homer, later call him to take issue with an episode that had aired. He said, "When the family car broke down in the desert, Homer shouldn't have made Marge carry that flat tire back to the gas station." The situation really bothered his father, prompting Matt to say, "Dad, this is a show where Homer skateboards off cliffs and strangles Bart and stuff, and that's what bothers you?"

His sister Lisa, on the other hand, loved her character, despite taking him to task over a few things. "She gets a little confused when her kids may imitate some of the behavior they see," he said with a laugh.

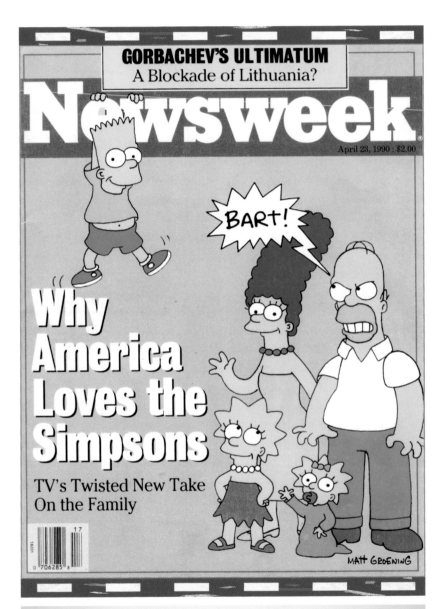

After becoming a huge national sensation, Matt's animated breakout hit, *The Simpsons*, graced the cover of the April 23, 1990 edition of *Newsweek*. © *Newsweek*.

During the event, Matt joked that every Monday morning FOX executives, whom he described as a "pretty dour bunch," danced in the halls after the overnight ratings came in. He always believed that if he ever got something on television that reflected what he imagined in his mind, he would be widely successful. "I came along at exactly the right time," he said. "I thought it was gonna be massive."

Matt was not far from the truth. Response from the early episodes washed over the network and entire *Simpsons* crew like a tidal wave and the show's sudden popularity was greater than anyone had imagined. That month, FOX was so pleased with the early results of the show they ordered a second season of 23 additional episodes to follow the original 13 set to air during the first season. Noting the series' rocketing success, FOX chairman Barry Diller proclaimed, "The show lights every fire of everybody who sees it."

Enhancing the show's image starting that season, Matt and company cooked up the idea of featuring celebrity guests as added attractions. Sam McMurray, a featured player on *The Tracey Ullman Show* and known for minor film roles in *Raising Arizona, National Lampoon's Christmas Vacation, L.A. Story, The Wizard,* and *C.H.U.D.,* was the first actor to lend his voice in the third episode of the first season, "Homer's Odyssey." Additional guest artists dropped in that year to provide vocal characterizations in subsequent episodes, including comedian Albert Brooks ("Life on the Fast Lane"), Kelsey Grammer ("Krusty Gets Busted), and Penny Marshall ("Some Enchanted Evening"). It would become the show's stock-in-trade, with many more top stars appearing on the program during its second season and beyond.

Another signature of the show that emerged during the first season was its ingenious, rib-tickling use of parody—from comical play on words in the titling of episodes (i.e., "Moaning Lisa," a comical take on the famous painting, Mona Lisa, or "The Crepes of Wrath," a spin on John Steinbeck's novel, *The Grapes of Wrath*) to jokes on pop culture, classic movies, and major historical events, from the 1960 Kennedy–Nixon debates to the L.A. riots. All of it became part and parcel of the *Simpsons'* universe.

LIVING IN STYLE

Early into the show's first season, with heir personal fortunes on the upswing, Matt and Deborah temporarily moved out of their tiny two-bedroom beach cottage in Los Angeles's eclectic Venice district into a scenic two-bedroom house overlooking the Pacific Ocean in the posh cliff-side community of Pacific Palisades. They had commenced tearing down their old place to build a much larger California bungalow-style, two-story home—that Deborah called "The House The Simpsons Built"—complete with touches of folk art, craftsman style architecture, and a canoe landing out back on the canal behind their home. There they would raise their son, Homer, and their second child on the way.

Like at their Venice house, Matt worked out of a studio in the garage of the Pacific Palisades place. Calling himself "the most semi-organized person I know," his greatest challenge was wading through packed Bekins boxes looking for materials he needed while working on his *Life in Hell* strip in an environment that seemed more cluttered than his regular studio, if possible. Pulling off the "starving artist" mentality in his strip these days was harder for him to fake convincingly. In his bachelor days, he mostly did strips about struggling and relationships, and these days "I do strips about kids," he said.

Despite most of his professional and financial dreams coming true, Matt has said it all was a "distant second" to the birth of his son. During his time at home, he enjoyed nothing more than watching baby Homer with his pacifier in his mouth speed across the hardwood floor in his child-sized walker ("Hey, Homer," he would joke, "Don't suck and drive.") and the spectacular sunsets and scenic ocean views from their grassy backyard together with Deborah and their son. While the prospects of fatherhood scared him a bit, he was having a good time with it knowing he would make mistakes—"different mistakes, and more benign ones"—than his parents did, with hope of a different outcome than his own childhood.

Proudly wheeling the energetic toddler around in his stroller, people burst out laughing every time after asking Matt what his name was and he replied, "Homer." They thought he was joking. "They'd get horrified looks on their faces," he said, "when they realized I wasn't kidding."

With Matt's twisted take on American family quickly becoming cultural icons, many catchphrases of his characters likewise caught on with audiences, from Homer's "D'oh!" to Bart's "Eat my shorts," "Don't have a cow, man!" and "Aye caramba!" The most enduring was Homer's drawn-out "D'oh!" The line was something Dan Castellaneta, the voice of Homer, improvised during a recording session. He borrowed the phrase—shortening it—from Scottish-born character actor James Finlayson's one-eye-squinting, slow-burn, double take of "Dooooooh!" he made famous in many classic Laurel and Hardy comedies in the 1930s and 1940s.

Interest in licensing the characters instantly mushroomed as well. By March of that year, FOX fielded 100 offers daily from parties wanting to license Matt's smash cartoon hit. Following a blizzard of publicity, FOX chairman Barry Diller discouraged the show's staff from doing any more articles for the time being, uneasy about "fueling too much hype before the series has taken a firmer hold." A toy company was already readying a talking Bart Simpson doll to unleash on the world. That February, a FOX executive showed Matt the first prototypes for the line of talking Simpsons dolls, including Bart. He promised, for any kid who pulled their string, the message would never come out in the same order. His only disappointment was "They wouldn't let him [Bart] belch."

Turning down many other offers, for fear of overexposure, Matt generally approved ideas for licensed merchandise that struck him as "crazy" and injected "a little anti-cuteness" into the marketplace. Thus, one product that met his approval was a Bart Simpson car air freshener. In gleefully discussing it, he said, "Most actual human beings would probably be appalled by being personified on a car air freshener. We don't have that problem."

By the end of the year, approximately 200 licensed products swarmed retailers across the country, including *Simpsons* key rings, puppets, talking toothbrushes, pajamas, and a poster of the troublemaking

Bart spouting the phrase, "Stay Outta My Room, Man!," that instantly sold out an initial printing of 250,000 copies. The first handheld Nintendo game issued by video-game maker Acclaim, *The Simpsons: Bart vs. the Space Mutants*, also became an instant bestseller. The surge in popularity of Matt's yellow-skinned, feuding family even provoked comedienne Tracey Ullman to half-joke that "next season we're going to appear as a live 30-second spot on *The Simpsons*." Once considered too radical for television, Matt's phenomenal success was an indication his characters, as the *New York Times* noted, had become "pure mainstream."

At times Matt, who turned 36 that year, found the implications of his characters' success overwhelming. "I didn't know what the ramifications of success would be," he said. Unlike his success with *Life in Hell*, then running in 200 newspapers, he admitted he was afraid to walk down the street seeing people wearing *Simpsons* T-shirts, fearful they might "beat me up . . . The people who are now my fans now frighten me."

While audiences had not tired of his eminently obnoxious TV cartoon brood, one thing Matt outgrew was his relationship with Pantheon Books, publisher of *Life in Hell* books, calendars, and postcard books that had sold 1.3 million copies to date. That month, he inked a reported seven-figure, multibook deal with Harper & Row as the exclusive publisher of *Simpsons* books, based on his number-one ranked FOX television show, as well as additional *Life in Hell* projects—an astonishing 15 projects produced over a three-year period—beginning in the fall. The first book to tie in with *The Simpsons* was a 350,000-copy first printing of a Christmas book based on the previous holiday special, "Simpsons Roasting on an Open Fire," along with a 100,000-plus first printing of a *Simpsons* postcard book. Thereafter, Matt would author a combination of *Life in Hell* and *Simpsons* projects and anything else he wanted.

BREAKING DOWN BARRIERS

Happily, *The Simpsons* became the sort of breakthrough comedy show Matt had long envisioned—one that succeeded by "crashing barriers."

During its first season, his series proved, as he believed, that cartoons were not just for kids, despite some ill-advised critics drawing comparisons between his befuddled cartoon family and the raunchy, rowdy Bundys on *Married . . . With Children.* "I suppose there's some similarity," Matt begrudgingly admitted. "I guess the big difference is that *Married . . . With Children* is more cartoony."

Some viewers took issue with the bad behavior and language used by the beer-bellied Homer (whose favorite beer label was Duff Beer) and squabbling siblings, Bart and Lisa. One young viewer wrote to Matt that his father "wouldn't let him watch because there [is] so much bad language and everybody hurts each other's feelings." Writer Jerry Lazar of *US* magazine went so far as to label Matt's bad-mannered family as "The Bratty Bunch," a far cry from the saccharine '70s TV clan *The Brady Bunch.* His relatively radical creations also drew a firestorm of criticism from principals, teachers, and child psychologists who frowned on the bad example the show set for young viewers. They were concerned over the widespread influence of Homer's infamous, underachieving son, Bart, a so-called "role model of rudeness" and known for his glibness ("Eat my shorts!"), on an entire generation of kids following his example.

That May, principals of Lutz Elementary School in Ballville Township, Ohio; Cambridge Elementary School in Orange, California; Taylor Mill Elementary School in Covington, Kentucky; and many others banned students from wearing in classrooms a T-shirt picturing a spiked-hair Bart with the slogan "Underachiever and Proud of It" emblazoned underneath. Others like Peggy Charen, president of Action for Children's Television, who sided with Bart and his creator, bemoaned, "How can you teach the Constitution if you ban T-shirts?"

Then United States Drug Enforcement Chief William Bennett even blasted the show and its poor message, though he later admitted to having never watched the show. Matt dealt with the controversy head-on, saying, "[Bart] has been labeled an underachiever and his response to that is that he's proud of it. He didn't call himself an underachiever. He does not aspire to be an underachiever." He added, "Kids are smarter than a lot of adults give them credit for. I feel sorry for authority figures who are troubled by kids having fun."

That first season, Matt and FOX found themselves in the enviable position of not having enough new episodes to satisfy their viewers. The network decided to purposely limit exposure of the series during "sweeps months" in May as it only had one episode left to broadcast before the start of the second season four months away. On April 1, after preempting the series, however, FOX was deluged by callers complaining about the show's absence. "I talked to one mother who said she used *The Simpsons* as a reward for her kids being good," Matt recalled. He added, "The kids complained that they had been good for nothing." Even merchandisers became uneasy over the prospects of the show not being on much or at all after its final episode. Matt, Brooks, and Simon seriously debated whether to rerun the show during the summer or simply vanish from the tube until the fall. As Matt stated at the time, "It's not a happy situation."

FOX decided to rebroadcast the series throughout the summer, giving audiences who had seen the show the first time around a second opportunity. At the end of May, in a bold move, FOX also announced plans to shift *The Simpsons* from Sunday to Thursday nights as part of its expansion to five nights the following season and to compete in the same time period against NBC's number-one rated sitcom for four straight years, *The Cosby Show*, which had slipped to number two during the past season. One uncertainty among media pundits was whether *The Simpsons* had the knockout punch to dethrone the prime-time comedy champion, or if it could "handle the heat . . . [and] Mr. Cosby," as Richard Zoglin of *Time* magazine wrote.

Nobody knew for sure, but, in the midst of widespread mania over Matt's American family at its wildest, the television industry was quick to nominate *The Simpsons* for three Emmy Awards that year. On September 16, Matt attended the live telecast of the 42nd Primetime Emmy Awards with his fellow *Simpsons* producers and voice cast. Also making their first personal appearance as presenters were the Simpsons themselves—accomplished by Klasky Csupo animators using

Matt beams proudly holding the first of many Emmy Awards he won for *The Simpsons.* © *Reuters.*

green-screen technology to matte them into the live setting—walking down the aisle of the Pasadena Civic Auditorium, where the annual awards show was held, to the podium on stage to present the Emmy for "Outstanding Lead Actor in a Comedy Series," won that year by Ted Danson of *Cheers*.

All of it was a sideshow to the most noteworthy moment of the evening: Matt winning his first Emmy Award for "Outstanding Animated Series (For Programming One Hour or Less)." In the years ahead, he repeated the honor nine more times. Clad in a tuxedo, he was all smiles afterward for a crush of photographers. The kid from Portland had indeed arrived.

Despite some second-guessing by critics over FOX"s decision to slot *The Simpsons* in head-to-head combat with *The Cosby Show* Thursday nights at 8:00 P.M., Matt's oddball nuclear family, which had finished in the weekly Nielsen Top 10 seven times and was ranked number-one as recently as late August, prevailed. After premiering on October 10, it trounced *The Cosby Show*, setting a series high record with 33.6 million viewers and ranking number-one for the week overall, compared to *Cosby*, which ended in sixth place with 28.5 million viewers, about 5.5 million viewers less, according to A.C. Nielsen Company. By the week ending November 9, Matt's off-the-wall creations, tied for eighth place with 27.4 million viewers, still bested *Cosby* in 10th place heading into the week of Christmas. As one critic opined, *The Simpsons* clearly had "raided Cosby's audience" and done damage to the popular NBC sitcom, which fell to fifth place overall from the previous season.

That season, with Matt's approval, the onslaught of *Simpsons* merchandise tie-ins continued. One that shook up the radio industry, thanks to record airplay, was the first Simpsons album, *The Simpsons Sing the Blues*. Released by Geffen Records in September 1990, the CD, featuring a defiant-looking, arms-folded Bart on the cover, made *Billboard*'s "Top 10 Pop Albums" chart and peaked at number three on the *Billboard 200* with over a million sales. Featuring mostly original music, except for "Moaning Lisa Blues" (from the February 11th episode, "Moaning Lisa") and six cuts in all, one of the most requested first tracks on North American radio stations—and first single released commercially only in the United Kingdom—was Bart's hard-hitting rap tune, "The Bartman," which was certified gold after selling more than 400,000 copies. Another popular tune featuring Bart was "Do the Bartman," anonymously written by pop star Michael Jackson.

On Halloween that year, Matt and company turned yet another page in the young franchise's history, airing its first *Treehouse of Horror* special. The half-hour anthology contained three separate, self-contained parodies of horror, science fiction, and the supernatural with The Simpsons somehow in the mix. Thereafter, it became an annual tradition.

Following such a landslide of acclaim and notoriety, after only two years on the air, the most pressing concern for Matt and his fellow producers was how to sustain that momentum—while handling the delicate balance between rising cult favorite and cartoon hit—without experiencing a thundering fallout before its time. That would pose some serious challenges for them in the months ahead, ones they hoped to avoid.

6

The Makings of a Television Classic

On Thanksgiving Day, 1990, Matt watched anxiously as an imposing 60-foot helium-inflated balloon floated down Fifth Avenue in New York City's annual Macy's Thanksgiving Day Parade. An enthusiastic throng of parade goers straddling opposite sides of the street cheered wildly as the familiar spiky-haired, yellow-skinned character of Bart Simpson, clad in orange shorts and blue tennis shoes, colorfully made its debut. Looking on as his troublemaking cartoon alter-ego towered over the parade route (something he described as "pretty wild"), Matt felt for the first time—it "really hit" him—that he had become a success.

He was not alone in that sentiment. Thanks to *The Simpsons*, FOX's goal of becoming a fourth network looked more feasible. Not only did the series generate millions in licensing revenue, with fans scooping up as many as one million authorized *Simpsons* T-shirts per week, but, more importantly, advertising revenue helped lift the network out of the red. With success, however, also came the added pressure to sustain it. Matt understood the inherent responsibilities of keeping the characters and show not just relevant, but also on top. As he stated, "Creating cartoons is like playing God. You create your own characters and their lives are entirely in your hands."

Bumped up 10 more episodes than their first season, Matt found producing the series for its second season much more intense. Everyone worked "like crazy," taking around 52 weeks to complete 22 episodes in a season. "So we have to figure out another solution," Matt stated then.

As one of the show's three executive producers, Matt remained a stickler when it came to quality. He wanted animation with enough depth, vivid characters, and situations that went beyond sitcom one-liners so adults would also watch it. Despite such a rigorous production schedule, midway into the second season, he was pleased by the end result. "We think we have something very special," he said. "If we can do good things with it, we'll do them. But we don't just want to do things to do them. Most of all, I'm in this business to have fun."

Public acceptance of *The Simpsons* went beyond character animation and humorous storylines. Americans were longing for a show that was realistic and projected the way the world really was, unlike happy family sitcoms of the past. Matt's series struck a common chord that many understood of leading unfulfilled lives and doing their best every day to survive. He also understood the connection. As Matt told the *Chicago Sun-Times*, "Part of the Simpsons appeal is the acknowledgment that you can still love the people who drive you crazy."

Changing positions in the weekly ratings war with *The Cosby Show* throughout the 1990–1991 season, FOX, which had gained a reputation of airing crasser programs than other major networks, kept *The Simpsons* on Thursday nights until 1994, when it moved back to Sundays. Throughout its second-season run, many more critics jumped on *The Simpsons* bandwagon, calling it "the best-written sitcom of the year" and recommending that viewers give the cartoon "a chance" during summer reruns.

By its third season in 1991, with *Newsweek* dubbing them "TV's new first family," Matt's half-bent characters became, as one writer described, "a standard part of the American vernacular" that in no way lost its luster with audiences. In a year filled with many career triumphs, Matt's animation family again came in a distant second; Matt was then performing double-duty as a father after Deborah gave birth to their second child, another son, Abraham, named after Matt's grandfather.

Matt arrives in style flying on the Western Pacific Airlines Boeing 737 Simpsons jet in 1995. © *AP*.

Meanwhile, Matt's ratings-busting cartoon hit inspired a major animation boom on broadcast television, with the other major networks riding the coattails of its success by producing a glut of prime-time cartoon series pilots. Only two were made into series, neither successful: Steven Spielberg's *Capitol Critters*, airing in January 1992 on ABC, and Stephen Bochco and Hanna-Barbera's *Fish Police*, premiering in February 1993 on CBS. (Not picked up: *The Wayneheads*, a claymation series from *In Living Color*'s Damon Wayans; and *Cleveland City Limits*, based on Arsenio Hall's alter-ego rapper character, Chunky-A.) As one critic noted, ". . . the ONLY reason 'The Simpsons' are popular is because they're 'The Simpsons.'"

On January 21, 1992, Matt and company unceremoniously switched animation houses for *The Simpsons*, dropping the original start-up company, Klasky Csupo, in favor of Film Roman. During the run-up to the start of the third season, Matt, who had presided over all aspects of production, from scripts to storyboards to voice-overs to animation, eased off to devote more time to developing other projects. He still showed up ideally once a week at his office on the 20th Century Fox lot and Film Roman animation studios, 45 minutes away in North Hollywood, poking his head in on various stages of production and communicating mostly by fax or by phone. "I've got to say it's much more fun to visit the animators," he said, "because they're a lot happier than TV comedy writers."

Matt sat down with producers and the voice cast to read through each script with the writers after they were written to checkmark those lines that got laughs. "We'd retreat to the rewrite room, and spend a couple of days working on the script again," he explained. "Then on the following Monday, we read the script through one more time with the actors, after which most of the writers disappear back into the rewrite room and tighten it up, while the actors spend the rest of the day recording the script."

The Simpsons' writing team that pushed the show to more ambitious and complicated areas in its weekly storylines included brilliantly funny workaholic writers—and, as Matt called them, "a rare combination"—Mike Reiss and Al Jean. Others included Jon Vitti, George Meyer, Jeff Martin, John Swartzwelder, David Stern, Frank Mula, Jay Kogen, Wally Wolodarsky, and comedian Conan O'Brien (credited with writing four episodes) who left after the 1992–1993 season to succeed David Letterman as the host of NBC's *Late Night with . . ."*

LAUGHTER HAS ITS PRICE

On October 23, 1992, more than a month into its third season, Matt and FOX received some unwelcome publicity when comedienne Tracey Ullman, whose comedy/variety show FOX had cancelled in 1990, sued the network for profits from *The Simpsons*. Once stating, "I breast-fed those little devils," Ullman launched a suit claiming she was owed part of the lion's share to Matt's characters—whose popularity had outstripped that of her own series—since they had originated on her program. The multimillion-dollar lawsuit, *Ullman v. The Simpsons*, played out in Los Angeles Superior Court in front of a jury. Ullman contended she had a right to a share of revenues—estimated at $2.5 million of FOX's estimated $50 million in profits from merchandise—based on the terms a 12-page contract she had signed with the network just hours before filming the first episode of her show in February 1987.

FOX attorneys handling the case, Louis Meisinger and Rita Ruzon, represented that Ullman had "limited" creative control, that she was simply a hired performer, who was paid $3 million for the three-and-a-half seasons her show aired, and an additional $58,000 in royalties for *The Simpsons*, thereby having no claim whatever on merchandising rights to spinoffs. "Nobody [Ullman] gets that deal when they are performing as an actress on a series," Meisinger told the court.

Ullman testified that, although she was not involved in every aspect of her series, she defended keeping *The Simpsons* on the program to the show's writer-producer James L. Brooks. "I remember Jim once saying he thought the Simpsons were a little frightening," Ullman said in the courtroom. "And I said, 'No, they're very '80s. This is an '80s show. We've got to keep up with the times.'"

Despite her claim, the court eventually ruled in favor of the network.

The incident, though a major distraction, failed to diminish the public's enthusiasm for Matt's creations. One of the great watershed moments that season was his and the *Simpsons'* team's on-the-air dispute with then President George H. W. Bush, who was running for re-election, which only enhanced the show's stature as a cultural icon. In a speech he delivered on January 27 to the National Religious Broadcasters Convention, Bush stated that ". . . the nation needs to be closer to the Waltons than the Simpsons. (Then First Lady Barbara Bush was equally vocal, once saying on record, "*The Simpsons* is the dumbest thing I've ever seen.") The former President made his remarks on a Monday and on the following Thursday, Matt and *The Simpsons'* team of writers, producers, and animators dreamed up a fitting response. With the country in the midst of an economic crisis, they added a new tongue-in-cheek opening to the January 30th rebroadcast of the episode "Stark

Raving Dad." They showed the bewildered Simpsons watching Bush on television deriding them with his now-famous remarks, and with Bart spouting, "Hey, man, we're just like the Waltons. We're both praying for an end to the recession." That year, Bush was defeated by the Democratic candidate, former Arkansas governor Bill Clinton.

Later in 1996, during the show's seventh season, long after Bush was out of office, Matt recorded an entire half-hour episode, "Two Bad Neighbors," in which the Bush family moved to Springfield right across from the Simpsons. It resulted in all-out war between the two families—with Homer shredding the ex-president's finished memoirs in an outdoor motor and Bush spanking Bart, who complained afterward to his dunderheaded dad, "I begged him to stop but he said it was for the good of the nation."

In future episodes, Matt took delight in skewering Republicans, something that predated the series. "Ever since I was a kid the Republican politicians have seemed like villainous buffoons," he later told *Playboy* magazine in 2007, "since Richard Nixon. He was such a cardboard villain. All of these guys since seem to be more of the same."

By 1993, with his financial status greatly enhanced as a result of his success, the long-haired, T-shirt- and sneaker-clad 39-year-old cartoonist was accused by many of his alternative newspaper friends of "selling out." Far removed from his days of driving a beat-up Datsun and now sporting a sleek new black BMW convertible and his own limo driver, he was not about to change a thing. "When I was a kid, my friends and I used to put on puppet shows, make comic books," he said with a shrug, "and I decided that's what I wanted to do, to play in every medium. I don't consider anything beneath me."

If anything, Matt felt his success helped him identify himself more closely to oppressed children when he was that age, sitting at their desks, waiting to cause trouble, and develop a spirit of solidarity with his two boys, Homer, then three, and Abe, then one year old, who he gladly spoiled, seeing things through their world. In fact, any time they took a trip to the toy store, the big-hearted, big-kid cartoonist always bought toys in threes—one for Homer, one for Abe, and one for himself to play with.

Fielding offers that season to develop a movie or another cartoon situation comedy, Matt found it difficult to choose. One project he was passionate about developing was a show starring *The Simpsons* fan-favorite and longtime host of Bart and Lisa's cherished fictional kid's show, *Krusty the Clown*. Matt had based Krusty partially on Rusty Nails, a popular television clown from his hometown, and designed him to look like Homer Simpson with clown makeup. That season, the burnt-out, dissolute clown starred in the finale—setting a record with a lineup of guest celebrity voices, including Johnny Carson, Hugh Hefner, Bette Midler, Luke Perry, the Red Hot Chili Peppers, and Elizabeth Taylor—called, "Krusty Gets Kancelled." Many fans also lobbied for Matt to turn his highly popular characters Itchy and Scratchy, super-violent versions of cat-and-mouse characters he grew up with like Hanna-Barbera's Tom and Jerry and Pixie and Dixie, into their own half-hour show. But Matt resisted, saying that "my feeling is less is more. Once you've skinned and flayed a cat, ripped his head, made him drink acid and tied his tongue to the moon, there really isn't much to say."

Reflecting on the state of the industry at the time, Matt declared how proud he was of *The Simpsons* for opening the door for animation to take "more chances" on television. Until his series' arrival, cartoon shows were mostly homogenous, assembly-lined kinds of characters, plots, and voices. Thanks to *The Simpsons*, the landscape of television changed, populated by a new wave of minimalist animation fare with a distinct look, including *Ren & Stimpy*, *Beavis and Butt-Head*, *South Park*, and others, none of which looked like "the same old thing."

Behind the scenes, however, all was not well in *The Simpsons* universe. Conflicts erupted in producing the show that season. Sam Simon, one of the show's original developers and creative supervisors for the first four seasons, was reportedly constantly at odds with Matt and James Brooks, a relationship that Matt once described as "very contentious." Eventually, Simon, who former *Simpsons* director Brad Bird described as "the unsung hero" of the program, left the show in 1993 over so-called "creative differences." Simon, who negotiated a deal including a share of profits every year and onscreen credit as an executive producer, earns

$10 million a year from *The Simpsons,* despite not working on the series since his departure.

That year, Matt expanded his empire by cofounding with Cindy and Steve Vance and Bill Morrison his own comic book company, Bongo Comics Group (named after the character, Bongo, in his strip, *Life in Hell*). Matt serves as its publisher. In launching the imprint, he stated, "I'm trying to bring humor into the fairly grim comic book market. I'm not a big fan of solemnity and I wanted to inject a little humor for kids into the market. There's plenty of great, very funny stuff being done for immature adults, but there's nothing smart and funny for kids out there."

As a result, everything Matt published was kid-friendly. The first titles he issued were *Simpsons Comics,* including a series of annual, all-original stories, including *Treehouse of Horrors,* based on *The Simpsons'* yearly Halloween specials. Other new series he published included *Radioactive Man, Itchy & Scratchy, Bartman, Lisa Comics,* and *Krusty Comics.* (The imprint later published comic books based on Matt's *Futurama* series and a crossover comic combining *The Simpsons* and *Futurama,* called *Futurama Simpsons Infinitely Secret Crossover Crisis.*) During the company's first year of operation, they were recognized with the prestigious Diamond Gem Award for best new publisher of the year and the Will Eisner Award for best short story for "The Amazing Colossal Homer."

The success of Bongo Comics led to Matt's creation of Zongo Comics, an imprint of Bongo, in 1994, whose sole purpose was to publish comics for more "mature readers." Under this imprint, he started with a line of *Jimbo* comics, created by his close friend and legendary artist Gary Panter, and expanded that line to include comics by other cartoonists like Mary Fleener's *Fleener* series. In creating his second comic-book company, Matt just wanted to give adult readers another choice. "I can understand given the following we have with Bongo and the intensity of some of the fans that some people will buy anything with the name on it, and I won't want a little kid to pick up an underground-type comic that we published and be warped for life," he said with a laugh.

Matt displays a copy of the first special collector's edition in 1993 of *Simpsons Comics and Stories* featuring Bartman (alias Bart Simpson) on the cover.

Starting with the 1994–1995 season, FOX picked up *The Simpsons* for another three years. That fall, besides dominating Sunday night television, the series, entering its sixth season, was rebroadcast nightly in national syndication. Overall, Matt felt the reruns gave loyal viewers and newcomers a chance to see the show from a different perspective. "We try to put so much in every episode that they change when you see them again," he explained. "One of the other aims that we have for this show is to make them hold up to repeated viewing." With added exposure through syndication, he was hopeful of seeing kids who grew up watching the series rewatching it as adults for another 10 or 15 years and thinking, as he put it, "'Oh, my goodness, I didn't realize that there's a whole other level.'"

MAINTAINING SUCCESS

Despite ruling over an empire that included a thriving television cartoon series, a bitingly hilarious syndicated comic strip, and two comic-book imprints, during *The Simpsons* sixth season, Matt stuck his nose in where he felt he could "improve the show." While the half-hour sitcom was a smooth-running and well-oiled operation, with bright and highly skilled people at every level, he saw his job as making sure "we maintain the soul of the show," he said. "Sometimes you can't see the forest for the trees and I try to nudge the show so it will keep on track. Sometimes it works and sometimes it doesn't."

While sometimes the finished shows were not always as good as he hoped they would be, Matt was happy overall with the direction. Occasionally, in an attempt to preserve the integrity of the characters, he dealt with what he called the "sleazy, behind-the-scenes stuff" that went on in making the show, butting heads with the network over exploiting *The Simpsons* in "creepy ways," believing because they were a cartoon "you can do anything." As he explained, "I try to make the guys who smoke cigars realize that it's in their own interests to keep the show top-notch and not exploit it and run it into the ground. Sometimes I'm successful, sometimes I'm not."

One major disagreement erupted that season over Matt's opposition to James L. Brooks producing a March 5, 1995, crossover episode

Matt makes a personal appearance in 1995 at Hollywood's Name That Toon gallery joined by a larger-than-life version of his cartoon hellion, Bart Simpson. *(Courtesy: Raymond Cox.)* © *Raymond Cox. All rights reserved.*

that season with *The Critic,* a half-hour cartoon series about a pudgy, wisecracking New York film critic, Jay Sherman (voiced by Jon Lovitz). Also produced by Brooks's company, the series, created by former *Simpsons* executive producers Al Jean and Mike Reiss, who had left *The Simpsons* after the fourth season. *The Critic* had jumped to FOX after being cancelled on ABC. The episode "A Star Is Burns" from the sixth season of *The Simpsons* was intended to generate interest in *The Critic.* The basis of Matt's argument was that viewers would "see it as nothing but a pathetic attempt to advertise *The Critic* at the expense of *The Simpsons,*" and possibly imply he had created or produced *The Critic,* as erroneously reported in many newspapers. Unable to stop its production, Matt ultimately asked that his name be removed from the opening credits. Brooks complied. Afterward, Matt publicly criticized the multiple Emmy-winning veteran coexecutive producer, saying the episode "violates the Simpsons' universe."

Brooks was nonplussed over Matt airing his grievances to the press. "I am furious with Matt," he stated, "...he's allowed his opinion, but airing this publicly in the press is going too far. ...his behavior right now is rotten."

Ruffling a few feathers by his actions that season, Matt once again attempted to launch new ideas he had been brewing. One such project was a live-action *Krusty the Clown,* featuring the snarly, chain-smoking kiddie show host from *The Simpsons.* The project never took off, nor did two other pitches he made: *Young Homer* and a show starring non-Simpsons citizens from the town of Springfield.

Matt has acknowledged that despite going through many writers since the first season, *The Simpsons'* continued success was greatly due to the writing staff remaining faithful to his vision of a family, who, despite their dysfunctional and goofball behavior, were actually a healthy, loving family unit underneath. Mocking the controversy that had resulted when the character J. R. Ewing was shot on the top-rated CBS prime-time drama, *Dallas,* the May 21, 1995, season finale cliffhanger was indeed *Dallas*-esque, with nearly every Springfield citizen getting a chance to settle a score with the sinister nuclear-plant owner, Mr. Burns, in "Who Shot Mr. Burns?" As executive producer David

Mirkin, who replaced Sam Simon beginning with the fifth season, recommended to viewers in an interview before its airing, "We advise you to tape it and go through it frame by frame, not unlike the Zapruder film [the famous home movie of President John F. Kennedy's assassination], and see if you can come up with a theory of who shot Mr. Burns and why."

Becoming one of the most-watched episodes in the show's history, viewers had to wait until the September 1995 seventh season premiere to learn the answer to the question, with producers taking every precaution to safeguard the secret. "We planted some misleads along the anima-

Original autographed drawing of Matt's beer-bellied, doofus dad, Homer Simpson.

tion assembly line," Matt remarked in an interview, "so that even if someone sneaks a peak, they're in for a rude surprise."

High interest spilled over to the September 17, 1995, season-opener with the brainy Lisa exposing the identity of the would-be assassin. Audiences learned that the crusty, old Mr. Burns had survived, but had not learned anything from his near-death experience. The new season marked the addition of two new executive producers, Bill Oakley and Josh Weinstein, who had written episodes for previous seasons, and the exit of David Mirkin. Matt and his fellow producers carried the suspense into the series annual *Treehouse of Horror* anthology. Using computer animation to transform *The Simpsons* "in a way you've never seen them before," they placed a computer-generated Homer in the real world after he was sucked through a "black hole" from the second to third dimension. One of the other high points of the season was

Rumors of going to the big screen began even before *The Simpsons* became the longest-running animated prime-time show on television, but it took many more years before Matt could attend the Los Angeles premiere of the long-awaited *The Simpsons Movie* in 2007. © *UPI.*

the appearance of former Beatle Paul McCartney and his wife Linda, a lifelong vegetarian, in dual guest roles in the season's fifth episode, "Lisa the Vegetarian," espousing the importance of vegetarianism. When offering veggie advice to Lisa, Homer remarks, "Rock stars—is there anything they don't know?" The fourth highest-rated show on the FOX network the week of its airing, the episode was subsequently honored with two awards—an Environmental Media Award and a Genesis Award—for highlighting environmental and animal issues.

By *The Simpsons'* eighth season in 1996, the show featured some 60 characters to draw from at any time in scripting new stories. Costs had skyrocketed dramatically, however, to twice as much as the cost of a live-action sitcom episode—around $1.5 million per animated episode compared to about $800,000 per live sitcom episode. The program took no less of a commitment to make—with staff members spending 15 hours a day, 51 weeks a year to come up with new material and maintain the same standards and quality that audiences had come to expect. Matt was well aware of what audiences liked. "The jokes are on different levels," he said. "Everyone loves the physical humor, then the pseudo-intellectuals like some stuff, and then there are butt jokes that appeal to my kids. I love it when people are all pretentious about it."

That season, Matt suffered a great personal loss that devastated not only him, but also his entire family. On March 15, 1996, losing his battle with cancer of the lymph system, his father, Homer, died. He was 76. Surviving the war hero, advertising pioneer, and filmmaker was his wife Marge, his daughters Patty, who still lived in Portland; Lisa, who made her home in Glendale, California; and Maggie, who resided in New York City; and his sons Mark, then based in Salt Lake City, and Matt, as well as seven grandchildren.

Recovering from the loss and with television placing tremendous demands on his time and energy, Matt continued drawing his *Life in Hell* comic strip but instead did it almost exclusively as single panels or 16-panel grids, becoming increasingly autobiographical. Thanks to the changing content of television becoming more provocative and open, Matt's popular strip had become "safe enough for a number of newspapers to print," as he said, without him having to tone it down at all, other than no longer resorting to profanity.

Midway into its ninth season in 1997, Matt's landmark series did something no other cartoon show had done in 31 years. On February 7, *The Simpsons* reached an historic milestone, overtaking *The Flintstones* as television's longest-running animated prime-time series with the airing of its 167th episode, "The Itchy & Scratchy & Poochie Show," starring those ultra-violent cat and mouse renegades. As broadcast television's newest toon titan, that spring, *The Simpsons* were featured on a second best-selling recording, *Songs in the Key of Springfield*, released by Rhino Records, and a year later, Matt authored the first official compendium about the series, *The Simpsons: A Complete Guide to Our Favorite Family*, for HarperCollins.

The significance of these events was not lost on Matt. Not one to rest on his laurels, he had more ideas up his sleeve, which he hoped to unleash on an unsuspecting public with the same dynamic results.

Spinning Off into the Future

In lockstep with network trends of producing offbeat and off-the-wall cartoon shows, Matt kept pace. He fulfilled a longtime fantasy of producing a kooky, animated science-fiction show. Ever since he was a kid, he had been a fan of the genre, having read old sci-fi magazines and gawking at their garish covers. He thought it would be "fun" to do an animation version of the books and magazine covers he loved so much growing up.

As early as 1993, Matt broached with FOX executives the idea of producing a follow-up series to *The Simpsons*. In September 1994, he generally discussed the concept. He said it would be "science fiction satire" and "fun to take advantage of a show that would have lots of explosions and mutants and robots that was also funny. What *The Simpsons* is to *The Flintstones*, this would be to *The Jetsons*."

Two years later, on March 25, 1996, Matt officially announced his plans to produce the not-yet publicly named series about a futuristic family from another planet expected to join FOX's lineup in 1997. Sparing much detail, one FOX executive confessed, "Matt Groening is a perfectionist, and he doesn't want to go ahead with a project until it's completely up to his standards."

While talks were open-ended, with only one year remaining then on his previous three-year *Simpsons* deal, Matt was also considering other options—still doing a *Krusty the Clown* television show and possibly a *Simpsons* movie. This was besides juggling producing his *Life in Hell* strip and books, Bongo comics, and, of course, *The Simpsons*. Rebounding after a slight ratings slump in its seventh season against CBS's *Cybill*, NBC's *Mad About You*, and ABC's *Lois & Clark* on Sunday nights, the show ranked number one with teens, age 12 to 17, and adults, 18 to 49.

First pondering his science-fiction idea, Matt dug back into his past. He reacquainted himself with many classic literary science-fiction novels he had enjoyed reading as a kid—H. G. Wells, Robert Heinlein, Philip K. Dick, Cordwainer Smith, Theodore Sturgeon, and Robert Sheckley—besides more modern contemporary works by writers like Neil Stephenson and Rudy Rucker. He spent many months researching the genre and made "long lists" of the kinds of characters and ideas he wanted to explore. Crediting everything from George Orwell's futuristic novel, *1984*, and films and television shows like *Star Wars* and *Star Trek* as inspirations, he penned a few hundred pages of material before meeting with fellow *Simpsons* writer/producer and science-fiction lover David Cohen, who he said had "a great knowledge of science and mathematics."

Conspiring over sci-fi movies, sci-fi books, 1980s computer games, vintage sci-fi magazines, and old TV shows like *Lost in Space* and *Doctor Who*, Matt and Cohen talked at length about what the series might be like. Going beyond Matt's original treatment, they devised a so-called epic space opera, *Futurama*. It was the story of a 25-year-old pizza delivery boy, Philip J. Fry, who accidentally gets frozen in a cryogenics lab on New Year's Eve 1999 and wakes up 1,000 years later in the 31st century to a different world in "New New York," built over the ruins of the original city after an alien invasion. As an intergalactic courier delivering packages throughout the universe, he befriends a sexy, "kickass," one-eyed alien woman trained in martial arts, Leela; a corrupt, cigar-smoking, porno-addict robot, Bender (a kind of robotic Homer Simpson); and a neurotic, lobster-like physician, Dr. John A. Zoidberg.

Five years after preliminary discussions with FOX, Matt's animated look into the future became a reality. In April 1998, he won a commitment from Peter Roth, then president of FOX Entertainment, after convincing him and others during their very first meeting on the show's merits after making his rather simplistic pitch: "This is *The Simpsons* in the future. It's new and original."

Actually, the meeting lasted three hours as he and Cohen extensively presented the show's concept. Matt suggested to Roth if FOX wanted to "own Sunday night, put *Futurama* between *The Simpsons* and *The X-Files*." Later Matt joked they saw "dollar signs" dance in front of their eyes. Roth ordered 13 episodes of the series on the spot. But, according to Matt, "Our first meeting was our last good meeting . . . that's when the honeymoon was over."

Afterward, FOX executives, in his words, completely "freaked" out. They complained that the show was "too dark" (taking issue in particular with the idea of coin-operated suicide booths) and "mean-spirited." They thought they had made a tremendous mistake. They regularly interfered with production. They bullied Matt and Cohen, who were underfunded and understaffed, into changing the show. As Cohen said, "I was an inch from losing my mind. We were working seven days a week and all our waking hours on two series."

Matt made the best of a difficult situation. As he admitted before the show's premiere, "I resisted every step of the way. In one respect, I will take full blame for the show if it tanks, because I resisted every single bit of interference."

Produced in association with Glendale, California's Rough Draft Studios (owned and operated by former *Simpsons* animators), its first series for television, Matt's original plan was to set some episodes on Earth, some not, featuring characters who "don't really fit in" in the legislated conformity of the future. "They do what they want to do," he said. When asked if the series offered any message about "the value of validity and being true to oneself," Matt joked, "I can't believe I *have* a message."

If there was an underlying tone, he claimed *Futurama* was "satirizing" people's perceptions about reinventing themselves. Another

Title card featuring the pizza-turned-intergalactic delivery boy, Philip J. Fry and friends, Bender the Robot, and sexy one-eyed alien, Leela, from Matt's futuristic animated series cocreated with David X. Cohen, *Futurama*. © FOX. *All rights reserved.*

prevailing theme was if "you were able to leave the here and now and go to the far future," he asked, "would you be able to reinvent yourself and be a completely different person or would you be the same loser you were before?"

Like the early days of *The Simpsons*, producing *Futurama* was a "painful process" for Matt. Because of budget restrictions and understaffing, writers were forced to work overtime. Matt wandered from one writing room to another, racing to meet pending deadlines. The collaborative process, in time, improved, but early on, writers ran into the same difficulties as did *The Simpsons* writing staff. "There are more jokes on the page, but there are no laugh tracks," Matt explained. "I think it's more difficult, in a way, than live-action."

In developing something unfamiliar to audiences, Matt and Cohen made the series' principal characters in their twenties so they could pursue more romantic and introspective stories about their fates and concerns about the future. To fill in space between characters and events, they created many new landscapes from scratch, based on one recurring question they and their staff had, "What are the rules of the universe?"

They agreed it was important *Futurama* had "a level of realism." They planned to place limits on what the characters did to ground the series so audiences responded to them on a human level. As for their lazy, lying, stealing, beer-drinking robot character, Bender, they worked around network censors to avoid him becoming "a bad role model for kids."

Unlike overly upbeat science-fiction cartoons and dark futuristic feature films, *Futurama* was to offer an alternative for viewers—"a mix of the wonderful and horrible"—featuring usual sci-fi conventions such as death rays, annoying robots, and hideous mutants. The stories, however, would essentially focus on the trials of being a young adult as seen through the character of Fry. Endlessly amazed by what he sees, this easily distracted voyager, stuck in a 20th-century mentality, bumbles through the future coming across as something of a loser, a character Matt believed audiences would identify with. "The Force is definitely not with him," Matt mused.

In developing *Futurama*, Matt gave kudos to Cohen for having much to do with the final direction of the show. "It's not my show, it's very much a shared vision with David Cohen and the animators and actors and writers on the show," he stated. "To really get the full take on *Futurama*, other than watching it, is to talk to David and the animators and all the writers, because this thing is big."

After advanced screenings, FOX executives complained that *Futurama* was "nothing like *The Simpsons*." Matt immediately came to its defense, "Yes it is. It's new and original." He instinctively knew he could never outdo *The Simpsons*, not even with *Futurama*. "I won't. I can't. Nothing can," he told a reporter. "I just hope every review isn't *Futurama* is no *Simpsons*. It's not a horse race."

Nonetheless, Matt never lost his enthusiasm, even if FOX had. In the end, he was hopeful his loyal followers and lovers of science fiction like himself embraced his wry, sci-fi opus. "I think the show's going to really amuse fans of science fiction," he told *Newsweek*, "because what science-fiction fans put up with is just disgraceful."

FLYING THROUGH ADVERSITY

That same month, Matt celebrated yet another important milepost in his career: publishing his 1,000th *Life in Hell* strip, syndicated weekly to 250 newspapers, a remarkable feat for something he originated, never thinking it would be published. Even after drawing the strip for 19 consecutive years, he still produced many of them at the last minute, saying, "It's horrible to be on deadline, facing a blank sheet of paper every week, but it's the only way I'm able to work."

After working on two huge collaborations each week, *The Simpsons* and *Futurama*, with more than 100 writers and animators, he still considered it "fun" to sit down and to "do something that is just mine, for which I can take full credit or blame," he said. "At least, even after all this time, I have the ability to keep my hellish existence alive and kicking."

During the first season of *Futurama* in 1999, Matt's 13-year marriage to Deborah ended. The two separated, with Deborah continuing to live in the Venice beach house they once shared. Eventually filing for divorce, Matt began seeing dating-expert Lauren Francis, a relationship that lasted for six years. Of the breakdown of his marriage, Matt stated then, "The demise of a family is unbelievably painful, to a degree I hadn't anticipated, and the amount of lingering grief can't be quantified." He added that he had thought "everything was on track" with his marriage and on its way to lasting for a long time, and never expected to suddenly be living alone. "I suppose the one interesting thing about this turn of events in my life," he said, "is that it really is an opportunity to reinvent myself."

FOX renewed *Futurama* for a second season. For Matt, though he knew the series would never repeat the success of *The Simpsons*, it was important to him that what he did was "honorable and fun." One reason he put the show so far out into the future was so nobody could say "we were wrong." As he remarked, "By the time 1984 came around, [George] Orwell's book seemed quite mild and everyone said, 'So?'"

On June 9, 2000, nearly six months after *The Simpsons* were awarded their very own star on the Hollywood Walk of Fame, Evergreen State College's most famous graduate returned. Matt delivered a sentimental commencement speech to the 1,244 new graduates. Having turned down numerous requests over the years to speak at commencements, he accepted his alma mater's invitation without hesitation. Once again donning his school's cap and gown, he expressed how genuinely pleased he was to be back on campus. Waxing nostalgic, he started off by noting, "As Bart Simpson would say, 'Aye, caramba!'" In the course of his speech, between quoting his work and sentiments of his life, he advised graduates on the importance of laughter. Quoting Homer Simpson, he said, "Laughter is what separates us from the animals. Except the hyenas."

Since leaving Portland in 1977 to launch his career, Matt, who still considers himself an Oregonian, faithfully returns to his roots, two or three times a year, to see old friends, visit his high school alma mater, and attend class reunions and has attended all of them so far. He readily admits he does not consider himself Lincoln High's "most illustrious graduate." He awards that honor to the late Mel Blanc, the longtime voice of Bugs Bunny and many other characters, and attributes much of his creative genius and astounding success to the place he once called home. "In a way, I feel the humor I'm known for definitely comes from growing up in Portland," he said, adding, "I love Portland."

Between May and June 2001, Matt's divorce from Deborah was made final. Moving into a new beach house in Malibu, Matt shared custody of their two sons, Homer (who goes by "Will"), then 12, and Abe, 9. Many friends often complained how appalling his parenting

Matt shares a laugh with fellow animation sensation Seth McFarlane, creator of FOX's *Family Guy* and *American Dad!,* at the All-Star Winter TCA Party in January 2007.

skills were, particularly how undisciplined he was as a parent. Matt admitted he was "a really bad example" and knew how much he annoyed "the hell out" of other parents, but he considered himself the dad he always wished he had had and tried to let his kids have "a good time." As he stated in a published interview, "My kids talked back to me and I laughed it off. Now they tell me I'm not funny anymore. My son said he wishes Seth MacFarlane [creator of TV's *Family Guy*] was his father."

Despite taking its share of critical lumps in the beginning, Matt's *Futurama* became beloved by members of the industry. During its original network run, the show was nominated five times for Emmys for "Outstanding Animated Program (For Programming One Hour or Less)" in 1999, 2001, 2002, 2003, and 2004, winning once in 2002. The 2002–2003 season marked the show's fifth and final season. FOX subsequently cancelled the series, becoming Matt's first program ever to be terminated.

Surprisingly, after its cancellation, *Futurama* enjoyed a remarkable renaissance, thanks to strong DVD sales and high ratings on Cartoon Network, which had begun rebroadcasting the series in January 2003 as the centerpiece of its late-night *Adult Swim* cartoon block. It had acquired exclusive syndication rights to the series for a reported $10 million. The tremendous sales and ratings of the old shows captured the attention of network executives at Comedy Central. In October 2005, following the expiration of Cartoon Network's contract, Comedy Central bought cable syndication rights, in what was called the largest and most expensive acquisition in the network's history, to reair the entire 72 episodes of *Futurama* starting in 2008.

In the course of negotiations, FOX, which controlled the rights to the series, suggested one better: Creating new episodes. After Comedy Central committed to producing 16 all-new episodes, the decision was made instead to produce four straight-to-video productions: *Bender's Big Score* (2007), *The Beast with a Billion Backs* (2008), *Bender's Game* (2008), and *Into the Wild Green Yonder* (2009), the latter meant to act as the series finale. Between March 23, 2008, and August 30, 2008, each subsequently aired in groups of four-part episodes—a total of 16 half-hours in all—on Comedy Central.

Matt, meanwhile, expressed a strong interest in continuing *Futurama* in some form, even as a theatrical film. As he told CNN, "We have a great relationship with Comedy Central and we would love to do more episodes for them, but I don't know...We're having discussions and there is some enthusiasm but I can't tell if it's just me." On June 9, 2009, Comedy Central made it official. They picked up *Futurama* for 26 new episodes to begin airing in mid-2010.

Despite some dips in its overall nightly ratings, his cartoon juggernaut, *The Simpsons*, remained a staple on FOX's Sunday night lineup. Matt had big-

Matt as he appears in animated form in his space-epic spoof, *Futurama*.

ger ideas still for his blue-collar characters—including plans for a theme park, his answer to Disneyland. "It'd be great!" he told *Face* magazine. "You'd have Simpsons Island, with a 600-foot statue of Homer. They'd sell donuts and beer in his head."

By 2003, with more than 300 episodes of *The Simpsons* having aired, Matt's greatest worry was making the show work without "repeating" themselves. One noticeable change was the public's acceptance of the show, particularly its unusual characterizations and themes that sometimes bordered on the edge of good taste. Even he was alarmed, however, when the show took on some very peculiar "Oh, my God, we can't do this. We can't do this" themes, as he put it. Fortunately, his worst fears never materialized. Unlike the series first season in 1989, when virtually everything they made drew the public's ire, the show's current audience seemed "eager to be offended," he once said, and those that were bothered by the program had tuned out.

Occasionally, the show stirred up controversy. Case in point: In one particular episode, Homer was watching an anti-drinking commercial that stated, "Warning! Excess consumption of alcohol may cause liver damage and cancer of the rectum," to which he dopily replied, "Mmmm . . . beer." The network wanted them to drop the scene since one of FOX's biggest advertisers was beer manufacturers. After the writer of the episodes tracked down a study supporting the claim, the network left it in.

ENJOYING IT AS LONG AS IT LASTS

How long will *The Simpsons* last? It's anybody's guess. Matt thinks the end will come one of these days, but, for now, it does not seem to be in sight. "I think what could eventually kill it," he told an Australian journalist in 2000, "is that it will get too expensive to be produced, but maybe we'll do movies—we've been talking about that."

That year, Matt had a similar conversation with James L. Brooks about the future of the series. Matt said, "You know, we can just sit around, and make the show run another couple of years. Or, we can actually make a 10-year plan."

Brooks simply replied, "Ten years."

Production of the show had not gotten easier; if anything, it was more difficult. But, should they suddenly lose their direction, then Matt felt "we should give it up." At the time, he said: "My goal has always been to make the people who like whatever I do really like it. To be fanatically devoted to it. The way to do that is have a strong point of view and deliver the goods. What I'm most proud of about the show is that we reward you for paying close attention. I still catch stuff I didn't catch before."

Besides keeping the show alive, Matt voiced his belief it was time to produce *Simpsons* movies beginning that year. The greater task was figuring out how to "justify" taking the show to the big screen. "We probably

Matt speaks at the invitation-only Simpsons ride crew party at Universal Studios Hollywood in May 2006.

could put out just about anything," he said, "and some people would come. But we want to honor the fans."

For many years, rumors of *The Simpsons* first full-length feature were ultimately squashed each time Matt was asked in interviews about the prospects of bringing the series to movie screens. In April 1994, when a reporter questioned him again, he said, ". . . I doubt it will happen. I would love it. I'm ready to do it any time, but no one can agree on how to divide up the obscene profits so there won't be any profits [laughs]."

Two years year later when asked again, Matt kept everyone guessing. "Yeah, someday, but anything involving signing a new contract with *The Simpsons* means that people involved with producing the show come out of nowhere, and it's hard to read the contracts after the saliva is wiped off because everyone's drooling for the immense amount of money they think they're entitled to," he said. "I imagine it's highly unlikely we'll ever do one. It's a shame because there should have been two or three movies by now."

Work on a script for a feature-length version began in 2001, after the voice cast was signed to star in a film based on the television show. Even then, Matt and his fellow producers fretted over the impact doing a movie would have on its crew, especially focusing on doing two projects at once—a film and weekly television series.

Finally, in April 2006, television's longest-running sitcom's first big-screen feature, *The Simpsons Movie*, entered production. Slated for theatrical release in July 2007, the film, in which Homer accidentally pollutes Springfield's water supply and he and his entire family become wanted fugitives, planned to follow the series' 20th anniversary and broadcast of its 400th episode that season. Done in the same style of the series, the movie's screenplay, coscripted by Matt, Brooks, Ian Maxtone-Graham, George Meyer, David Mirkin, Mike Reiss, Mike Scully, Matt Selman, John Swartzwelder and Jon Vitti, underwent more "revisions than Joan Rivers' face," wrote journalist Michael Mallory (reportedly over 100 different drafts, including making the film as a musical), during its production, which took 18 months to complete. As Matt said of the first film in the franchise's history, "When we started the TV show back in 1989, we tried to reinvent the rules of television animation, which is to make changes much further along in the process than is usually done. We've done the equivalent of that in the movie." His desire was for the film to be dramatically stronger than the television series, giving die-hard fans and loyalists "something that you haven't seen before."

Prior to its release, 20th Century Fox Studios sponsored a nationwide competition of 16 Springfields across the United States. The town of Springfield, Vermont, a small hamlet, won the honor to host the film's world premiere. On July 21, the theater rolled out the "yellow

Matt relishes some frosting during ceremonies celebrating the historic 400th episode of *The Simpsons. (Courtesy: Fanpix.)*

carpet" (instead of the traditional "red") welcoming Matt, members of the voice cast, and life-sized costumed characters of *The Simpsons* to mark the movie's debut. Three days later, an advance premiere was held in Los Angeles.

On July 27, 2007, showing nationally on 5,550 screens at 3,922 movie theaters, the eagerly awaited PG-rated, 87-minute adventure raked in $30.7 million on its opening day in the United States. It became the 22nd highest single-day gross in box-office history, and took in a combined $74 million its first weekend, making it the fifth-highest of all time for a weekend-opening in July. The 20th Century Fox release outperformed the studios' own projections—of $40 million—upon its release. By the end of the year, the production's total domestic gross topped $183 million, and more than $527 million worldwide.

Critics were equally enthusiastic about *The Simpsons'* first major movie event. As *Variety* critic Brian Lowry enthused: "If somebody had to make a *Simpsons* movie, this is pretty much what it should be—clever, irreverent, satirical, and outfitted with a larger-than-22-minutes plot, capable (just barely) of sustaining a narrative roughly four times the length of a standard episode."

Following the film's extraordinary success, the remarkable resiliency of *The Simpsons* franchise continued unabated. Matt would help celebrate more milestones in the years ahead. In May 2008, he and longtime *Simpsons* executive producer James L. Brooks took the first-ever trip, along with Los Angeles Mayor Antonio Villaraigosa, actress Lisa Kudrow, actor Kelsey Grammer, Universal Studios president and CEO Ron Meyer, Universal Studios Parks & Resorts chairman/CEO Tom Williams, and Universal Studios Hollywood president and chief operating officer Larry Kurzweil, on the new Simpsons simulator ride at Universal Studios Hollywood, which simultaneously opened that month at Universal Studios Florida. In April 2009, as part of 20th Century Fox Studio's year-long celebration, dubbed "Best 20 Years. Ever," Matt and members of the voice cast unveiled and autographed five new Simpsons U.S. postage stamps, featuring the likenesses of Homer, Marge, Bart, Lisa, and Maggie. Of the honor, Matt joked, "This is the biggest and most adhesive honor *The Simpsons* has ever received."

Matt takes the first-ever trip on the new Simpsons Ride opening in May 2008 at Universal Studios Hollywood with (front row, left to right) Matt, Los Angeles Mayor Antonio Villaraigosa, actress Lisa Kudrow, actor Kelsey Grammer, and (back row, left to right), Universal Studios president and chief operating officer Ron Meyer, Simpsons executive producer James L. Brooks, Universal Studios Parks & Resorts chairman and chief executive officer Tom Williams, and Universal Studios Hollywood president and chief operating officer Larry Kurzweil. *(Courtesy: BPI Entertainment News Wire.)*

That July, at the annual Comic-Con International convention in San Diego, the Guinness Book of World Records also honored him for the series becoming the longest-running sitcom after overtaking his childhood favorite, *The Adventures of Ozzie and Harriet* (the former champ with 435 episodes) during its 20th season. Later that month, he joined others to honor Japanese cartoon legend Hayao Miyazaki at the

Matt autographs a Simpsons-themed U.S. Postal Service stamp in May 2009 at the 20th Century Fox studios lot. © *AP Photo*.

Matt accepts a Guinness World Record certificate honoring *The Simpsons* for overtaking his childhood favorite, *The Adventures of Ozzie and Harriet*, as the longest-running sitcom in television history during its 20th season. *(Courtesy: World News Syndicate.)*

Academy of Motion Picture Arts and Sciences 13th Marc Davis Celebration of Animation, hosted by Pixar animation icon John Lasseter, at the Samuel Goldwyn Theater in Beverly Hills.

While over the years his characters' success has spawned many imitators, Matt understands *The Simpsons'* place in American culture and their universal appeal. "The show illustrates how you can live with the craziness of the contemporary family and tolerate people who drive you

Matt stands with fellow animation icons John Lasseter and Hayao Miyazaki in July 2009 at the Academy of Motion Picture Arts and Sciences' celebration of Miyazaki's incredible career at the Samuel Goldwyn Theater in Beverly Hills. (*Photo by Todd Wawrychuk*) © *Academy of Motion Picture Arts and Sciences.*

mad," he said. "'The Simpsons' are out of their minds and cause incredible grief, but love each other. You can look at them and go, 'As bad as my life is, it isn't that bad.'" Despite once being criticized by some as bad role models, he believes the show has taught a good message to kids, especially that "authorities don't always have your best interest in mind."

If Matt could give aspiring writers or animators any advice, it is to "do what makes you laugh." As he once explained, "Don't try to make other people laugh. It's something that took me a long time to learn. I didn't start making any progress in my work until I gave up the idea of trying to write jokes that would make other people laugh and just started doing work for myself, because that's when you start writing from the heart, and then people will get it, strangely enough, and they will respond to it much more strongly."

With his yellow-skinned, bug-eyed, dysfunctional family now part of the American lexicon, the 56-year-old cartoonist/animator/producer appears content with his legacy, although he is more apologetic about unleashing his mischievous Bart upon the world after raising two sons old enough to quote him and tell him "how annoying he is." His long locks of hair and beard now speckled with gray, Matt told an interviewer, "Being rewarded for what I used to be discouraged from doing is probably the best revenge of all. If I hadn't lucked out, maybe I'd be in an insane asylum. But even if I were in a straightjacket, I'd still be doodling with a crayon in my mouth."

After formerly driving his teachers crazy and dreaming his assaults on moral authorities and cultural absurdities would someday pay off, this self-assured creator of television's most enduring and beloved sitcom and cartoon family has indeed left a deep and lasting mark on American, pop culture. His influence, no doubt, will be felt for generations. Between elevating new standards and changing the course of animation and television, and winning almost universal acclaim in the process, he will be remembered, much to his chagrin, as a far better cartoonist than writer for his subversive and edgy humor that took him from spitballs to Springfield and, most of all, as the guy who created those lovable yellow lunks, The Simpsons.

SELECTED RESOURCES

Charlie Rose—Matt Groening and James L. Brooks/Christine Quinn (Charlie Rose, 2007)

The popular PBS talk-show host interviews *The Simpsons'* creator Matt Groening and executive producer James L. Brooks on his July 30, 2007, show to tie in with the theatrical release of *The Simpsons Movie.*

Futurama: Monster Robot Maniac Fun Collection (20th Century Fox Home Video, 2005)

This 88-minute one-disc collection includes four classic episodes from Groening's futuristic series—"Hell Is Other Robots," "Anthology of Interest I," "Roswell That Ends Well," and "The Sting," plus several bonus features, including introductions by Groening and executive producer David X. Cohen before each episode, and optional commentary from Groening, Cohen, and the show's voice cast for "Hell Is Other Robots."

The Simpsons: Bart Wars (20th Century Fox Home Video, 2005)

Released on May 17, 2005, to coincide with the theatrical debut of *Star Wars Episode III: Revenge of the Sith,* this nearly two-hour special features four complete episodes: "Dog of Death," "Marge Be Not Proud," "The Secret War of Lisa Simpson," and "Mayored to the Mob."

The Simpsons: Christmas (20th Century Fox Home Video, 2003)

This 92-minute disc features the 1989 Christmas special that launched the series, "Simpsons Roasting on an Open Fire," and four other classic yuletide episodes, "Mr. Plow," "Miracle on Evergreen Terrace," "Grift of the Magi," with Gary Coleman voicing a Tiny Tim-like character, and "Magi," featuring Krusty the Clown.

The Simpsons Movie (20th Century Fox Home Video, 2007)

This DVD features *The Simpsons* in their first and only full-length feature.

The Simpsons: The Complete First Season (20th Century Fox Home Video, 2001)

This three-disc DVD set encompasses 13 first-season episodes (1989–1990) and additional bonus material, including original scripts for four episodes ("Bart the Genius," "Bart the General," "Moaning Lisa," and "Some Enchanted Evening"), early sketches, stills and magazine covers, and much more.

The Simpsons: Treehouse of Horror (20th Century Fox Home Video, 2003)

This Halloween-themed anthology of this annual trilogy consists of four complete half-hour shows aired since 1989: *Treehouse of Horror V* ("The Shining, "Time and Punishment," and "Nightmare Cafeteria"); *Treehouse of Horror VI* ("Attack of the 50-Foot Eyesores, "Nightmare on Evergreen Terrace," and "Homer3"); *Treehouse of Horror VII* ("The Thing and I," "The Genesis Tub," and "Citizen Kang"); and *Treehouse of Horror XII* ("Hex and the City," "House of Whacks," and "Wiz Kids").

SELECTED BIBLIOGRAPHY

"And on the Seventh Day Matt Created Bart." *Loaded Magazine.* August 1996.

Angell, Jamie. "Explaining Groening—One on One with the Sultan of Fun." *Simpsons Illustrated* Vol. 1, No. 9 (Summer 1993): 22–30.

Barron, James. "A Sax Craze, Inspired by 'The Simpsons.'" *The New York Times,* January 14, 1996, pg. E. 2.

Beale, Lewis. "Tracey Ullman Blends Ditziness, Intellect to Perfection—She's Wacky, Endearing—and a Star." *Daily News of Los Angeles,* May 29, 1987, Valley, L.A. Life section, 1.

Bensoua, Joe. "Fox Beefs Up Its TV Lineup with Two New Shows." *Daily Breeze,* March 3, 1987, Entertainment section, C1.

Constantine, Peggy. "Wouldn't Batman Be Surprised?—Comic Books Become Trendy." *Chicago Sun-Times,* May 18, 1986, 30.

Deneroff, Harvey. "Matt Groening's Baby Turns 10: A Look at Who Helped Make 'The Simpsons' Work for Primetime." *Animation Magazine,* January 2000.

Doherty, Brian. "The Creator of 'The Simpsons' on His New Sci-Fi TV Show, Why It's Nice to Be Rich, and How the ACLU Infringed on His Rights." *Mother Jones,* March/April 1999.

Duncan, Andrew. "I'm an Incurable Neurotic. No Comedy Comes Out of Being Well Adjusted." *Radio Times* (UK), September 18–24, 1999.

"For Alternative Artists, Drawing Takes Backseat to Search for Ideas." *Chicago Sun-Times,* May 25, 1986, 8.

Gates, Anita. "Groening's New World, 1,000 Years From Springfield." *The New York Times*, January 24, 1999.

Gabree, John. "Books/Paperbacks New and Notable." *Newsday*, April 13, 1986, Books section, 12.

Green, Frank. "'Life in Hell' Is Lucrative for Artist." *San Diego Union*, August 3, 1985, 1-6, Lifestyle section, C-1.

Hauser, Susan G. "Mr. Groening's Neighborhood." *The Wall Street Journal*, October 27,1989, A28.

Holly, Rob. "The Simpsons' Father Speaks." *Cards Illustrated*, September 1994.

Infusino, Divina. "They're Absurd, They're Bizarre, They're Surreal, They're Morbid, They're Hostile, They're...New Wave Comics." *San Diego Union*, February 5, 1986, 1-6, Lifestyle section, D-1.

Isenberg, Barbara. *State of the Arts: California Artists Talk About Their Work*. New York: William Morrow, 2000.

Kim, John W. "Keep 'em Laughing." *Scr(i)pt*, October 1999.

McKenna, Kristine. "Matt Groening May Look Like Your Average Guy, But Remember, He's Got Homer and Bart Simpson Living in His Head." *My Generation*, May/June 2001: 48–52, 54.

O'Harrow, Robert. "Drawn from the Past." *Washington Post*, July 6, 1984, Final Edition, Style and Arts section, E7.

Paul, Alan. "Life in Hell." *Flux Magazine*, September 30, 1995.

Pendergast, Tom, and Sara Pendergast (editors). *St. James Encyclopedia of Popular Culture*. Detroit: St. James Press, 2000.

Racine, Marty. "The Crickets Take to Touring, Phil Collins Takes Exception, Record Firm Takes Action and Band Takes U.S. By Storm." *Houston Chronicle*, August 31, 1986, 2 STAR edition, Zest section, 10.

Reynolds, Pamela. "Binky Knows All." *Boston Globe*, September 18, 1986, Living section, 81.

Roderick, Kevin. "Revisiting Groening and the L.A. Reader," LA Observed.com, Available online. URL: http://www.laobserved.com/archive/2006/01/revisiting_groening_and_t.php.

Teer-Tomaselli, Ruth. "The Simpsons: What Do Sit-coms Tell Our Children About Gender?" *Agenda* No. 22 (1994): 52–56.

Tucker, Ernest. "New Breed of Cartoonists Draws Home on Funny Pages." *Chicago Sun-Times*, May 25, 1986, Sunday Living section, 8.

Wyley, Annemarie. "'The Simpsons' Creator Groening Grows Up." *Reuters*, September 3, 1999.

Zahed, Ramin. "Groening's Life No Longer Hellish." *Daily Variety*, January 15, 2000, A4.

INDEX

ABOUT THE AUTHOR

Photo courtesy: Brian Maurer.

Jeff Lenburg is an award-winning author, celebrity biographer, and nationally acknowledged expert on animated cartoons who has spent nearly three decades researching and writing about this lively art. He has written nearly 30 books—including such acclaimed histories of animation as *Who's Who in Animated Cartoons*, *The Great Cartoon Directors*, and four previous encyclopedias of animated cartoons. His books have been nominated for several awards, including the American Library Association's "Best Non-Fiction Award" and the Evangelical Christian Publishers Association's Gold Medallion Award for "Best Autobiography/ Biography." He lives in Arizona.